Quantile Methods for
Stochastic Frontier Analysis

Other titles in Foundations and Trends® in Econometrics

Performance Analysis: Economic Foundations and Trends
Valentin Zelenyuk
ISBN: 978-1-68083-866-4

Experimetrics: A Survey
Peter G. Moffatt
ISBN: 978-1-68083-792-6

Climate Econometrics: An Overview
Jennifer L. Castle and David F. Hendry
ISBN: 978-1-68083-708-7

Foundations of Stated Preference Elicitation: Consumer Behavior and Choice-based Conjoint Analysis
Moshe Ben-Akiva, Daniel McFadden and Kenneth Train
ISBN: 978-1-68083-526-7

Structural Econometrics of Auctions: A Review
Matthew L. Gentry, Timothy P. Hubbard, Denis Nekipelov and Harry J. Paarsch
ISBN: 978-1-68083-446-8

Quantile Methods for Stochastic Frontier Analysis

Alecos Papadopoulos
Athens University of Economics and Business
papadopalex@aueb.gr

Christopher F. Parmeter
University of Miami
cparmeter@bus.miami.edu

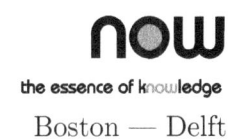

now

the essence of knowledge

Boston — Delft

Foundations and Trends® in Econometrics

Published, sold and distributed by:
now Publishers Inc.
PO Box 1024
Hanover, MA 02339
United States
Tel. +1-781-985-4510
www.nowpublishers.com
sales@nowpublishers.com

Outside North America:
now Publishers Inc.
PO Box 179
2600 AD Delft
The Netherlands
Tel. +31-6-51115274

The preferred citation for this publication is

A. Papadopoulos and C. F. Parmeter. *Quantile Methods for Stochastic Frontier Analysis*. Foundations and Trends® in Econometrics, vol. 12, no. 1, pp. 1–120, 2022.

ISBN: 978-1-63828-094-1
© 2022 A. Papadopoulos and C. F. Parmeter

All rights reserved. No part of this publication may be reproduced, stored in a retrieval system, or transmitted in any form or by any means, mechanical, photocopying, recording or otherwise, without prior written permission of the publishers.

Photocopying. In the USA: This journal is registered at the Copyright Clearance Center, Inc., 222 Rosewood Drive, Danvers, MA 01923. Authorization to photocopy items for internal or personal use, or the internal or personal use of specific clients, is granted by now Publishers Inc for users registered with the Copyright Clearance Center (CCC). The 'services' for users can be found on the internet at: www.copyright.com

For those organizations that have been granted a photocopy license, a separate system of payment has been arranged. Authorization does not extend to other kinds of copying, such as that for general distribution, for advertising or promotional purposes, for creating new collective works, or for resale. In the rest of the world: Permission to photocopy must be obtained from the copyright owner. Please apply to now Publishers Inc., PO Box 1024, Hanover, MA 02339, USA; Tel. +1 781 871 0245; www.nowpublishers.com; sales@nowpublishers.com

now Publishers Inc. has an exclusive license to publish this material worldwide. Permission to use this content must be obtained from the copyright license holder. Please apply to now Publishers, PO Box 179, 2600 AD Delft, The Netherlands, www.nowpublishers.com; e-mail: sales@nowpublishers.com

Foundations and Trends® in Econometrics
Volume 12, Issue 1, 2022
Editorial Board

Editor-in-Chief

William H. Greene
New York University
United States

Editors

Manuel Arellano
CEMFI Spain

Wiji Arulampalam
University of Warwick

Orley Ashenfelter
Princeton University

Jushan Bai
Columbia University

Badi Baltagi
Syracuse University

Anil Bera
University of Illinois

Tim Bollerslev
Duke University

David Brownstone
UC Irvine

Xiaohong Chen
Yale University

Steven Durlauf
University of Chicago

Amos Golan
American University

Bill Griffiths
University of Melbourne

James Heckman
University of Chicago

Jan Kiviet
University of Amsterdam

Gary Koop
The University of Strathclyde

Michael Lechner
University of St. Gallen

Lung-Fei Lee
Ohio State University

Larry Marsh
Notre Dame University

James MacKinnon
Queens University

Bruce McCullough
Drexel University

Jeff Simonoff
New York University

Joseph Terza
Purdue University

Ken Train
UC Berkeley

Pravin Trivedi
Indiana University

Adonis Yatchew
University of Toronto

Editorial Scope

Topics

Foundations and Trends® in Econometrics publishes survey and tutorial articles in the following topics:

- Econometric Models
- Simultaneous Equation Models
- Estimation Frameworks
- Biased Estimation
- Computational Problems
- Microeconometrics
- Treatment Modeling
- Discrete Choice Modeling
- Models for Count Data
- Duration Models
- Limited Dependent Variables
- Panel Data
- Time Series Analysis
- Latent Variable Models
- Qualitative Response Models
- Hypothesis Testing
- Econometric Theory
- Financial Econometrics
- Measurement Error in Survey Data
- Productivity Measurement and Analysis
- Semiparametric and Nonparametric Estimation
- Bootstrap Methods
- Nonstationary Time Series
- Robust Estimation

Information for Librarians

Foundations and Trends® in Econometrics, 2022, Volume 12, 4 issues. ISSN paper version 1551-3076. ISSN online version 1551-3084. Also available as a combined paper and online subscription.

Contents

1	Introduction	3
I	**Where We Are**	**9**
2	The Relation Between Conditional Quantiles and the Regression Function	11
3	Basics of Quantile Regression: The Independence Case	23
4	Where Quantile Regression and Stochastic Frontier Analysis Clash	33
5	Reconciling Quantile Regression with Stochastic Frontier Models	45
6	Likelihood-Based Quantile Estimation	53
II	**What We Can Do**	**59**
7	The Corrected Q-Estimator	61
8	Quantile-Dependent Efficiency	69

9	From the Composite Error Term to Inefficiency: A Fundamental Result	**79**
10	Quantile Estimation and Inference with Dependence	**87**
11	An Empirical Application	**97**
III	**For the Road**	**109**
12	Challenges Ahead	**111**
13	Summary and Concluding Remarks	**121**
	References	**123**

Quantile Methods for Stochastic Frontier Analysis

Alecos Papadopoulos[1] and Christopher F. Parmeter[2]

[1]*Athens University of Economics and Business, Greece; papadopalex@aueb.gr*
[2]*University of Miami, USA; cparmeter@bus.miami.edu*

ABSTRACT

Quantile regression has become one of the standard tools of econometrics. We examine its compatibility with the special goals of stochastic frontier analysis. We document several conflicts between quantile regression and stochastic frontier analysis. From there we review what has been done up to now, we propose ways to overcome the conflicts that exist, and we develop new tools to do applied efficiency analysis using quantile methods in the context of stochastic frontier models. The work includes an empirical illustration to reify the issues and methods discussed, and catalogs the many open issues and topics for future research.

Keywords: Conditional quantile function; quantile regression; deterministic frontier; inefficiency; stochastic noise; heteroskedasticity; non-linear quantile estimator

---

Alecos Papadopoulos and Christopher F. Parmeter (2022), "Quantile Methods for Stochastic Frontier Analysis", Foundations and Trends® in Econometrics: Vol. 12, No. 1, pp 1–120. DOI: 10.1561/0800000042.
©2022 A. Papadopoulos and C. F. Parmeter

1

Introduction

This monograph seeks to merge two seemingly disparate econometric fields, quantile estimation and stochastic frontier analysis (SFA). Why might these two fields be viewed as disparate? Quantiles exist on a continuum of the distribution, the frontier is a fixed object of it. As will be seen, these two approaches can, when used properly, be merged to provide a unified approach to studying a stochastic boundary.

The use of distribution quantiles for estimation purposes is an old story. The most well known case is the use of the sample median to estimate location parameters instead of the sample mean. More generally, sample quantiles are more robust than sample means against outliers, and this advantage has always been championed, in the face of contaminated samples that did not conform with the idealized conditions needed for sample means to fully perform as theory tells us that they should.

In econometrics, "quantile regression", introduced by Koenker and Bassett (1978), has become the most popular method to use quantile methods in estimation. With hindsight, it was a package with two interconnected but distinct offerings. The first offering was a new estimator focused on linear regression analysis that required no distributional assumptions, was more robust than least-squares methods with respect to outliers in the data, and, when the regressors were independent from the error term, allowed one to estimate consistently the slope regression coefficients. We will call it the "Q-estimator" henceforth, and "quantile regression" will also refer to their approach. We will use the term "quantile estimation" to refer more generally to approaches that pursue their inference goals by estimating quantiles.

The second offering was based on the fact that the Q-estimator could estimate the effects of regressors at different quantiles of the conditional distribution of the dependent variable, simply by choosing the probability associated with each quantile. In the case where the error term of the regression was independent from the regressors, this multiple-quantiles view gave rise to changes only in the value of the constant term of the regression. But when some form of dependence is present between regressors and the error term (like heteroskedasticity), the marginal effects of the regressors differ at different quantiles of the dependent variable, and the Q-estimator was able to provide this much richer information, making the least-squares estimator to suddenly look like a poor relative.

This is the "quantile approach" to statistical analysis and econometric inference proper, where a statistical aspect of our data, the conditional quantiles of the dependent variable, are mapped to an important structural aspect. To provide a prototypical example, if the dependent variable is earnings, and the regressor is a government subsidy program for professional education, "different effects at different quantiles" would tell us whether it was the low-earners or the high-earners that tended to benefit most from the policy. This multiple-quantiles estimation can be achieved by the Q-estimator and it is no wonder that it spread and saw intense use in the treatment effects literature. It remains today a methodology of choice when one wants to drill down on marginal effects and policy evaluation.[1]

In the process, the quantile regression toolkit expanded to include non-linear setups and quantile regression models that accounted for

---

[1] We take here the opportunity to note that our work will be focused solely on conditional quantile methods. The "unconditional quantiles" approach made widely known by Firpo *et al.* (2009) is beyond the scope of this work.

endogeneity, while its basic incarnation has become a standard feature of most econometric software, that makes it an off-the-shelf choice even for beginners ... which does not always lead to valid outcomes.

SFA, on the other hand, which begun with Aigner *et al.* (1977) and Meeusen and van den Broeck (1977), attempts to discern a stochastic boundary of firm performance, usually cost or output. These methods are not interested in average behavior, but in both an idealized level of performance and any deviations from it. This puts the model, and its corresponding estimators, at odds with traditional regression. However, it has connections to conditional quantiles as the frontier exists somewhere in the output space.

The application of quantile methods in SFA has in the past been rather sparse, but a recent flurry of interest in combining the two was what motivated the present work. We have four main goals: the first is to examine whether, and to what degree, the popular and easily available Q-estimator and quantile regression align well, or not, with the special properties and goals of SFA. We warn the reader that the conclusions here will be partly negative: there exist certain fundamental incompatibilities that do not allow the Q-estimator to provide in stochastic frontier models (SFMs) what it provides in treatment effects studies. Our second goal is to offer an overview of how the quantile approach has been used up to now in stochastic frontier analysis, using quantile regression or likelihood-based analysis. This gives an acute picture of the aforementioned incompatibilities. Our third goal is to provide new and ready-to-implement tools that allow the valid use of quantile regression for efficiency analysis, including estimation of the frontier but also quantile-dependent (in)efficiency measures. Our fourth goal is to sketch avenues for future research and *name* the many prints that are not yet blue, which is done partly throughout the text but also compiled in the penultimate Section of this work.

Sections 2 to 6 present the current state of affairs. We start in Section 2 by detailing the very close link between the regression function and the conditional quantile function, in order to show that the quantile relation is not some disconnected statistical aspect that lives independently of our regression specification. This section also shows what the quantile approach and the Q-estimator actually do, and we contrast this with what SFA models *want* to do, using also a simulated example. Already we encounter the first points of tension between the quantile regression approach and the SFA view.

The reader may be disappointed that we will not provide a detailed treatment here on the use of quantile approaches in the sister field of data envelopment analysis (DEA). This is intentional. The presence of stochastic noise makes the treatment of SFA and DEA distinct, and there are subtle, nontrivial complications that warrant a more thorough discussion of SFA methods due to the presence of both noise *and* inefficiency. We provide a heuristic discussion of this difference at the end of Section 2 to illustrate the main intuitive distinction of the stochastic and deterministic frontier models when quantile methods are applied.

In Section 3 we present the main characteristics and properties of the linear Q-estimator when the error term is independent of the regressors, as a necessary preparation to move to Section 4, where we show how some of these properties are fundamentally incompatible with the goals and purposes of SFA. Essentially, the area of friction is the quantile probability of the deterministic component (DF) of the stochastic frontier (SF).[2] To make the point forcefully, we include in this section a review of applied SFA studies that have used quantile regression, and we show how this incompatibility undermines the reliability and usefulness of their results. Section 5 begins the healing process: we discuss recent advances that properly construct the deterministic frontier.

Section 6 is where we move away from quantile regression, and we present likelihood-based approaches that use density functions that include as one of their parameters the probability of the zero-quantile of their distributions. We focus on a specific incarnation of the Asymmetric Laplace distribution for the noise term in a composite error SFA specification. We examine both frequentist and Bayesian lines of research. The Bayesian approach appears to achieve the *desideratum* of obtaining different estimates of regression coefficients and of inefficiency

---

[2]The word "deterministic" is used to describe the component of the dependent variable that depends on variables traditionally treated as *decision* variables of the firm.

per quantile, but we clarify that this only reflects the interconnected estimation uncertainty that is inherent in Bayesian econometrics.

Sections 7 to 10 present a new estimator, but also metrics and insights that allow to fruitfully use the quantile approach in SFA. In Section 7 we show how one can use the Q-estimator together with additional assumptions in order to provide conceptually valid and useful estimation and inference results in SFMs. In Section 8 we present quantile-dependent measures of efficiency both at the sample level, and at the individual level, but also how the conditional quantiles of the distribution of inefficiency can be used to offer a picture of how individual efficiency scores are distributed around a chosen quantile of the efficiency distribution.

In Section 9 we prove a fundamental result: that positive and high values of the composite error term of production SFA models, are expected to co-exist with low inefficiency, in a concrete probabilistic sense. An analogous result holds for cost models: when the value of the composite error term is negative and large in absolute value, cost inefficiency is expected to also be low. We decided to separate and stress this result because, with minimum assumptions and certainly for the distributions that are the mainstays of stochastic frontier analysis, it allows us to gauge *individual* inefficiency based on estimated quantities like the residuals of the model.

Section 10 examines the case of dependence between the error term and the regressors or other covariates. We first discuss the issues that generally arise when "traditional" heteroskedasticity co-exists with a skewed and non zero-mean error term, and how we can obtain consistent estimation in such a case. We then examine the particular SFA setting of "determinants of inefficiency" situation, and we develop a non-linear quantile regression model for this setup.

In Section 11 we provide an empirical illustration that showcases the approach of the four previous Sections, and functions as a guide for detailed applied studies.

Section 12 includes a list of the various open issues as well as ideas and directions for future research, while Section 13 offers a short summary and a few parting thoughts.

Part I
Where We Are

2

The Relation Between Conditional Quantiles and the Regression Function

We will use F to denote a production function, C a cost function, and f a generic function. We will use G and g to denote distribution and density functions respectively, indexed appropriately.

Consider a general regression model,

$$y_i = f(\boldsymbol{x}_i; \boldsymbol{\beta}) + \varepsilon_i, \quad i = 1, \ldots, n. \tag{2.1}$$

To an economist, this represents an attempt to describe the causal relationship between the dependent variable and the regressors, because the task of economics is to formulate causal models. There is an ongoing discussion about the interpretation of the vector $\boldsymbol{\beta}$, and frequently it is asserted that regression models are "conditional mean" models, where the $\boldsymbol{\beta}$ coefficients relate to the partial marginal effects of the regressors on the conditional expected value of y, not on y itself.

In order to examine what interpretation we can give to the coefficients in a conditional *quantile* setup, we take here the view that the unknown regression $\boldsymbol{\beta}$ coefficients carry first and foremost true causal effects of the regressors on the dependent variable itself, and not on its conditional expectation.[1] If it so happens that $E[\varepsilon_i \,|\, x_i] = 0$, then $f(x_i; \beta)$ *coincides* with the conditional expectation function of y given the specific x's. But there is a different conditional expectation function for every set of regressors. This is the statistical view of the relation that shies away from causality and considers the relation to be, in principle, predictive rather than causal. But even if $E[\varepsilon_i \,|\, x_i] \neq 0$, we maintain that the β vector relates to a causal effect (whether it is feasible, or not, to estimate it accurately is a totally different matter).

Enter the quantile point of view. If the error term has a distribution function $G_{\varepsilon|x}$ conditional on the regressors, its conditional quantile function (CQF) is defined as $Q_{\varepsilon|x}(\tau \,|\, x) \equiv \inf\{\varepsilon\colon G_{\varepsilon|x} \geq \tau\}$, where $\tau \in (0,1)$ is some probability value. This is a generalized inverse that accommodates distribution functions with discontinuities as well. We will henceforth assume that the error term is a continuous random variable in which case the CQF is the usual inverse of the distribution function, $G_{\varepsilon|x}^{-1}(\tau)$, so

$$G_{\varepsilon|x}^{-1}(\tau) = Q_{\varepsilon|x}(\tau|x).$$

Next, we can associate any selected τ with the distribution function of the dependent variable. For every τ, and every x_i, we have a value in the support of the dependent variable y_i, denote it for now $y(\tau, x_i)$, such that it holds

$$\Pr(y_i \leq y(\tau, x_i) \,|\, x_i) = \tau \implies \Pr\left(f(x_i; \beta) + \varepsilon_i \leq y(\tau, x_i) \,|\, x_i\right) = \tau$$
$$\implies \Pr\left(\varepsilon_i \leq y(\tau, x_i) - f(x_i; \beta) \,|\, x_i\right) = \tau$$
$$\implies G_{\varepsilon|x}\big(y(\tau, x_i) - f(x_i; \beta)\big) = \tau.$$

But $y(\tau, x_i)$ is nothing else than the CQF of y_i, $Q_{y|x}(\tau|x_i)$. Inserting the obtained expression for τ into the inverse distribution function

---

[1] As Griliches (1957, p. 20) blandly put it "The major restriction of our framework lies in the fact that we must assume that something is 'true,' – we must specify our 'true' equation. In practice, we may have very little to go on. However, our work will have no statistical validity unless we are ready to stick our necks out and to assume that something is 'true'."

expression for the error term we have

$$G_{\varepsilon\,|\,x}^{-1}(G_{\varepsilon\,|\,x}(Q_{y\,|\,x}(\tau\,|\,\boldsymbol{x}_i) - f(\boldsymbol{x}_i;\boldsymbol{\beta}))) = Q_{\varepsilon\,|\,x}(\tau|\boldsymbol{x}_i)$$
$$\implies Q_{y|x}(\tau\,|\,\boldsymbol{x}_i) - f(\boldsymbol{x}_i;\boldsymbol{\beta}) = Q_{\varepsilon\,|\,x}(\tau\,|\,\boldsymbol{x}_i)$$
$$\implies Q_{y\,|\,x}(\tau\,|\,\boldsymbol{x}_i) = f(\boldsymbol{x}_i;\boldsymbol{\beta}) + Q_{\varepsilon\,|\,x}(\tau\,|\,\boldsymbol{x}_i). \qquad (2.2)$$

Equation (2.2) is the fundamental relation linking a regression function with conditional quantiles. Comparing the regression expression with the CQF, the first important conceptual realization is how closely related they are: both revolve around the same core, $f(\boldsymbol{x}_i;\boldsymbol{\beta})$, which is why estimating conditional quantiles can be an alternative way to arrive at the causal relation. The second thing to note is that the CQF brings in the forefront what is concealed in the regression function: the possible statistical dependence between the regressors and the regression error term, through $Q_{\varepsilon\,|\,x}(\tau\,|\,\boldsymbol{x}_i)$, and so the possible existence of "other effects" of the regressors on the dependent variable.

When the conditional *error* quantiles do depend on the regressors, the CQF puts initially a question-mark on the correctness of the postulated regression model as a causal relationship: if the error term and regressors are statistically associated, does this reflect a causal link that should ideally be reflected in the regression function, or, hopefully, it is a statistical dependence that reflects the existence of some confounding relation "only"? And regardless, does this dependence destroy desirable estimator properties? We will show in Section 10 that when $Q_{\varepsilon\,|\,x}(\tau\,|\,\boldsymbol{x}_i) \neq q_\varepsilon(\tau)$ (i.e., when the CQF of the error term does depend on the regressors) in general we have $E[\varepsilon_i\,|\,\boldsymbol{x}_i] \neq E[\varepsilon_i]$. In such cases one has to account for regressor endogeneity, except under special dependence schemes.

But assuming that the endogeneity issues have been dealt with, the quantile regression approach brings any regressor effects on the dependent variable that operate through the error term back into the picture, slice-by-slice. It appears that quantile regression can be really valuable when we have an error term that has some form of dependence with the regressors. And indeed these are the cases where quantile regression have been extensively used and offered new insights, especially related to policy evaluation. See for example the collection of empirical studies in Fitzenberger *et al.* (2002) but also a recent special issue of the journal *Empirical Economics* (Fitzenberger *et al.*, 2022).

If such dependence reflects an underlying causal relation running from the regressors to some component of the error term, then it is clear that the total effect of each regressor on the dependent variable is the "sum" of these two effects, through $f(\boldsymbol{x}_i; \boldsymbol{\beta})$ and $Q_{\varepsilon \mid \boldsymbol{x}}(\tau \mid \boldsymbol{x}_i)$. On the other hand, if the possible statistical dependence reflects a causal relation from some component of the error term to the regressors, then strictly speaking, the "causal effect" of the regressors on the dependent variable is carried solely by $f(\boldsymbol{x}_i; \boldsymbol{\beta})$, while what comes through $Q_{\varepsilon \mid \boldsymbol{x}}(\tau \mid \boldsymbol{x}_i)$ represents effects originating in these other influencing factors. But even in such a case, and to the degree that we have no data on these lurking components of the error term, for *predictive* purposes we would like to know the total marginal effects on the dependent variable that are associated with a given set of regressor-values, even if these marginal effects confound other forces also.

This is at the heart of the argument in favor of running "quantile regressions", and at different τ values, and especially in treatment effects models: what is the marginal effect of a labor market policy on different quantiles of the conditional wage distribution? What are the effects of a cancer drug at different quantiles of the conditional survival rate distribution? To cover both causal scenarios mentioned above, what is the total effect *associated* with the treatment variable at different conditional quantiles of the dependent variable?

Quantile regression models typically assume a formulation of the CQF as $Q_{y \mid \boldsymbol{x}}(\tau \mid \boldsymbol{x}_i) = \alpha(\tau) + \boldsymbol{x}_i' \boldsymbol{\beta}(\tau)$. Comparing this with Equation (2.2), we see that with such an estimating equation we confound in the estimated "quantile coefficients" the effect of the regressors through $f(\boldsymbol{x}_i; \boldsymbol{\beta})$, with their effects through $Q_{\varepsilon \mid \boldsymbol{x}}(\tau \mid \boldsymbol{x}_i)$. But *that is exactly our goal* – in treatment effects models, where quantile regression has been particularity popular.

When the error term is independent from the regressors and so $Q_{\varepsilon \mid \boldsymbol{x}}(\tau \mid \boldsymbol{x}_i) = q_{\varepsilon}(\tau)$, no "other effects" of the regressors exist, and the CQF provides no more information on the causal relationship than that provided by the regression function. In this case, quantile regression can be seen as a more refined *predictive* tool (forecasting, even) that pivots off the unique regression function and offers a more targeted prediction by focusing on a point of the stochastic distribution of the error term and by incorporating its probabilistic effect on the dependent variable. Nevertheless, Koenker (2005) himself repeatedly questions the value-added of quantile regression in the independence case, writing that "there would be little need" for it (p. 13), or even that it is "superfluous" (p. 74).

Stochastic Frontier Analysis Meets Quantile Regression

Enter SFA. In the SFA way of seeing things, $f(\boldsymbol{x}_i; \boldsymbol{\beta})$ is the deterministic frontier (usually its logarithmic transformation), and so Equation (2.2) clarifies that whatever effect the regressors (say, production inputs) may have on the conditional quantiles of the dependent variable through the conditional quantiles of the error term (and for whatever reason), these are conceptually *totally separate* from the deterministic frontier. Equation (2.2) is not a single equation, but many, one for each value of τ. But changing the value of τ does not change the deterministic frontier, which remains the same throughout all these relations. Looking at different quantiles of y does not mean looking at a different deterministic frontier, which is $f(\boldsymbol{x}_i; \boldsymbol{\beta})$ and remains unique.

Our use of the word "deterministic" is not to suggest that there is no error in the model or that firms do not face shocks. Neither does it imply that the inputs $\boldsymbol{x}_i$ are not treated as random variables. They are, but by the researcher. For the firm, they are decision variables, hence also the word "deterministic". So, the deterministic frontier is the bound that the firms face for their production plans. In a world without inefficiency, or shocks (namely, uncontrollable external influences), it would be the maximum output of the firm. Naturally this can change based on shocks, but in that case we have a stochastic boundary, hence the link to SFA. Again, for $f(\boldsymbol{x}_i; \boldsymbol{\beta})$ the deterministic frontier, the only movements around this bound are through shocks or inefficiency.

In SFA, the effects of the regressors through $Q_{\varepsilon \mid \boldsymbol{x}}(\tau \mid \boldsymbol{x}_i)$ are viewed autonomously, for two reasons: first they are treated as "indirect" effects, separate from the contribution of the regressors to the deterministic frontier. Here is an example from a production model: increasing quantities of the input "capital" increase the deterministic frontier value of the output. At the same time, they may crowd-out competitors and so observed output may tend to increase even more due to demand-side effects. We would not want this indirect effect to be estimated together with the contribution of capital in the deterministic frontier. A second reason to want to keep the effects represented through $Q_{\varepsilon\,|\,x}(\tau\,|\,x_i)$ separate, is that they may carry in them information about a possible relation between regressors and inefficiency. An example here is a higher level of the input "labor", that will tend to increase the deterministic frontier value of the output. But at the same time it may activate more intense regulation and public oversight, which can lead to an increase in inefficiency.

To show more tangibly how the goals of SFA are not a direct match to those of a standard regression or a treatment effects framework, we provide a simulated example. We consider the following data-generating mechanism,

$$y = \alpha + \beta x + \varepsilon, \qquad \alpha = 1, \ \beta = 0.5.$$

We generated 50,000 independent observations with four different error terms. In Model 1, $\varepsilon = v \sim N(0,1)$. In Model 2, we made the Normal error term conditionally heteroskedastic, setting $\varepsilon = (1+\gamma x)v$, $\gamma = 0.2$. Model 3 is a standard (cost) SFM, with a Normal-Half Normal error, $\varepsilon = v + u$, $u \sim$ HN (Half Normal), and Model 4 has a conditionally heteroskedastic SF error term, $\varepsilon = (1+\gamma x)(v+u)$, again with $\gamma = 0.2$. In all cases the regressor is independent from the error components v and u (which are themselves independent). In Table 2.1 we present the estimates across these four models for various quantiles along with the corresponding OLS estimates.

We induced heteroskedasticity in this way following Koenker and Bassett (1982). Specifically, for Model 2 say, the conditional quantile function of the dependent variable becomes

$$Q_{y\,|\,x}(\tau\,|\,x_i) = \alpha + \beta x + (1+\gamma x)q_v(\tau)$$
$$= (\alpha + q_v(\tau)) + (\beta + \gamma q_v(\tau))x.$$

So we have $\alpha(\tau) = \alpha + q_v(\tau)$, $\beta(\tau) = \beta + \gamma q_v(\tau)$, and these values constitute the probability limit of the Q-estimator.

Table 2.1: Least squares and quantile regression estimation results. Simulated example.

		\multicolumn{3}{c}{Q-Estimator}
Model	OLS	$\tau = 0.25$	$\tau = 0.50$	$\tau = 0.75$
$\alpha = 1$				
1: Homoskedastic	0.996	0.318	1.002	1.671
2: Heteroskedastic	0.995	0.313	1.005	1.671
3: SFA homoskedastic	1.791	0.993	1.772	2.562
4: SFA heteroskedastic	1.791	0.988	1.772	2.568
$\beta = 0.5$				
1: Homoskedastic	0.499	0.502	0.498	0.499
2: Heteroskedastic	0.499	0.370	0.496	0.634
3: SFA homoskedastic	0.500	0.502	0.499	0.497
4: SFA heteroskedastic	0.660	0.505	0.654	0.805

Model 1 is the prototypical linear regression model with spherical errors (or, it is Model 2 with $\gamma = 0$). OLS and the Q-estimator are consistent for the slope coefficient. Irrespective of the τ chosen, the Q-estimator gives the same estimate for the slope coefficient, and only the estimate for the constant term changes, due to changing $q_\varepsilon(\tau)$. In Model 2 we still have a zero-mean error term, but now conditionally heteroskedastic. Both estimators are consistent but here the Q-estimator offers much more. We learn that the *total* marginal effect associated with the regressor at quantile probability $\tau = 0.25$ is 0.37 and not 0.5 which is the value of β. This happens due to conditional heteroskedasticity. Note that in a real-world sample, we do not know the true value of β, but with quantile regression *it is not our goal* to find the true value of β. Our goal is to find the changing *total* marginal effects of the regressor at different quantiles of the dependent variable.

Model 3 is the cost SFM. Here OLS is consistent only for the slope coefficient, while the estimate for the constant term incorporates the expected value of the non-zero mean error. The Q-estimator is consistent for the quantile coefficients. Due to the absence of heteroskedasticity, the estimates for the slope coefficient are the same for all τ's. Model 4 has an SFA error term, with heteroskedasticity. Here OLS is inconsistent even for the slope coefficient. This happens because we have an error term that it is at the same time heteroskedastic *and* non-zero mean. The Q-estimator is consistent (for the quantile coefficients), and so the estimates we see are the total marginal effects of the regressor at the different quantiles, namely, we get estimates of $\beta + \gamma q_\varepsilon(\tau)$. But in SFA, *this is not our goal*: we want to estimate β separately, because it relates to the deterministic frontier, while $\gamma q_\varepsilon(\tau)$ is treated as a distinct effect that may have to do partly with inefficiency. So, even though valid results, these slope estimates are not what we want.

But even when the error term is independent from the regressors and $Q_{\varepsilon\mid x}(\tau \mid x_i) = q_\varepsilon(\tau)$, there is still information here on inefficiency and the distance from the deterministic frontier. Whatever the case is, $Q_{\varepsilon\mid x}(\tau \mid x_i)$ remains a distinct concept whose effects must be recovered separately from the deterministic frontier $f(x_i; \beta)$. Therefore the question of what could be the meaning of a "quantile-specific frontier" remains. We will have more to say about this in Section 4.

Already, we have identified a crucial conflict of SFA with the benchmark "quantile regression" approach. The latter consciously and deliberately estimates the two sources of regressor effects on the dependent variable as one. In SFA we want to estimate them separately. One could ask then "why not use a conditional mean model to estimate β on its own, and then run quantile regressions at different τ values to estimate the full effects, having the best of both worlds?" Well, we have just shown above by simulation that with an error term that is conditionally heteroskedastic *and* not of zero-mean, *OLS stops being consistent*. This is perhaps not very widely realized in the discipline, so we will provide the proof here.

Suppressing the observation index, consider the linear SFA regression model with conditional heteroskedasticity,

$$y = x'\beta + \varepsilon, \quad \varepsilon = \sigma(x)(v + u),$$

with v and u being independent of the regressors, while also $E[v] = 0$, and $E[u] \neq 0$. In this model we have the asymptotic result

$$\begin{aligned}\operatorname{plim}(\hat{\boldsymbol{\beta}} - \boldsymbol{\beta}) &= \left(E[\boldsymbol{x}\boldsymbol{x}']\right)^{-1} E[\boldsymbol{x}\sigma(\boldsymbol{x})(v+u)] \\ &= \left(E[\boldsymbol{x}\boldsymbol{x}']\right)^{-1} E[\boldsymbol{x}\sigma(\boldsymbol{x})]E[v] + \left(E[\boldsymbol{x}\boldsymbol{x}']\right)^{-1} E[\boldsymbol{x}\sigma(\boldsymbol{x})]E[u] \\ &= 0 + \left(E[\boldsymbol{x}\boldsymbol{x}']\right)^{-1} E[\boldsymbol{x}\sigma(\boldsymbol{x})]E[u] \neq 0,\end{aligned}$$

because $E[u] \neq 0$. Moreover, we have that in general $E[\boldsymbol{x}\sigma(\boldsymbol{x})] \neq E[\boldsymbol{x}]E[\sigma(\boldsymbol{x})]$. If we could break this expected value like this, all the inconsistency would concentrate on the estimation of the constant term, even in the presence of non-zero mean inefficiency. But because we cannot, the combined effect of conditional heteroskedasticity and a non-zero-mean error, is to spread the inconsistency to the slope coefficients making OLS generally inconsistent in such a case.

Apart from the above serious issue, "multiple quantiles estimation" is ultimately not compatible with SFA on other grounds, as we will see in Section 4. In order to show this fundamental incompatibility, and more generally to examine how well quantile regression aligns with the special characteristics of SFMs, we must present the basic mechanics of quantile regression and the properties of the Q-estimator, and for the benchmark case where the error term is independent from the regressors. This will also lead us to make a distinction between quantile regression as an alternative framework for analysis and inference, and the Q-estimator as an alternative estimation tool "only". But before doing that, we venture into DEA territory to show why there the quantile approach does not encounter such issues.

The Quantile Approach in Data Envelopment Analysis

DEA has already enjoyed widespread application of quantile methods. With DEA, the lack of stochastic noise actually makes quantile methods more appealing, as boundary methods are known to suffer (sometimes markedly so) in the presence of outliers. Quantile methods can mitigate some of these adverse effects. See recent papers by Aragon *et al.* (2005), Daouia and Simar (2007) and Martins-Filho and Yao (2008) for prominent examples in this arena.

The notion of a production frontier of continuous τ-order, $\tau \in (0,1)$, coinciding with a τ-conditional quantile, is well developed in the DEA framework. For example, in Aragon *et al.* (2005) (and the deterministic quantile methods literature more broadly), each $\tau \in (0,1)$ has a direct interpretation as a quantile relative to the frontier, which is well-defined for $\tau \uparrow 1$. However, in the SF setting, given the presence of both u (inefficiency) and v (stochastic noise), this is no longer the case.

What makes quantile estimation of a stochastic frontier different than the deterministic frontier setting is that while for a given quantile, τ, in both frameworks we can certainly calculate $Q_{y\,|\,x}(\tau\,|\,x)$, inefficiency loses its meaning if it is not compared with the appropriate object. In DEA this object is the deterministic frontier, so every τ is with respect to this "limiting" frontier. However, in the SFA setting this is not the case because of the presence of v. Its existence does not allow one to take an arbitrary quantile τ and then make comparisons with the frontier. In the deterministic case, this works because without v the frontier is the logical limit as $\tau \uparrow 1$. But once v is present, the deterministic frontier, the maximal amount of output produced for a given level of the inputs, is no longer the logical limit as $\tau \uparrow 1$, but some intermediate value. Conditional on the regressors, any τ relates to the distribution of $v \pm u$. Therefore, a given τ, estimated as a *stochastic* frontier quantile, cannot be compared to the deterministic frontier.

To show this clearly using our notation, for a production DEA model with inefficiency $u \geq 0$, we have

$$y_i = f(\boldsymbol{x}_i) - u_i \implies \Pr\left(y_i \leq Q_{y\,|\,\boldsymbol{x}}(\tau\,|\,\boldsymbol{x}_i)\right) = \tau$$
$$\implies \Pr\left(f(\boldsymbol{x}_i) - u_i \leq Q_{y\,|\,\boldsymbol{x}}(\tau\,|\,\boldsymbol{x}_i)\right) = \tau$$
$$\implies \Pr\left(u_i \leq f(\boldsymbol{x}_i) - Q_{y\,|\,\boldsymbol{x}}(\tau\,|\,\boldsymbol{x}_i)\right) = 1 - \tau$$
$$\implies f(\boldsymbol{x}_i) = Q_{y\,|\,\boldsymbol{x}}(\tau\,|\,\boldsymbol{x}_i) + Q_{u\,|\,\boldsymbol{x}}(1-\tau\,|\,\boldsymbol{x}_i).$$

Because as $\tau \to 1$ we have that $Q_{u\,|\,\boldsymbol{x}}(1-\tau\,|\,\boldsymbol{x}_i) \to Q_{u\,|\,\boldsymbol{x}}(0\,|\,\boldsymbol{x}_i) = 0$ (since $u \geq 0$), we can express the DEA deterministic frontier as

$$\text{DEA: } f(\boldsymbol{x}_i) = \lim_{\tau \to 1} Q_{y\,|\,\boldsymbol{x}}(\tau\,|\,\boldsymbol{x}_i).$$

In stochastic frontier analysis where the model is enhanced with stochastic noise v, rearranging Equation (2.2) we have

$$f(\boldsymbol{x}_i) = Q_{y\,|\,\boldsymbol{x}}(\tau\,|\,\boldsymbol{x}_i) - Q_{\varepsilon\,|\,\boldsymbol{x}}(\tau\,|\,\boldsymbol{x}_i).$$

In order to obtain the deterministic frontier as the limit of the CQF of output, the τ value must tend to that value for which the CQF of the composed error term becomes zero. It is natural to denote this pivot value τ_{DF}: $Q_{\varepsilon|x}(\tau_{DF}|\boldsymbol{x}_i) = 0$, and we can write for the SFA deterministic frontier

$$\text{SFA:}\ f(\boldsymbol{x}_i) = \lim_{\tau \to \tau_{DF}} Q_{y|x}(\tau|\boldsymbol{x}_i).$$

Comparing the two, we see that in DEA the deterministic frontier is the limiting value of the CQF of output when τ tends to the fixed and known value "1", while in SFA the deterministic frontier is the limiting value of the CQF of output when τ tends to τ_{DF}, which is unknown, and must be estimated from the data.

To provide further insight of the importance of the deterministic frontier, consider now a production stochastic frontier model in levels,

$$Y_i = F(\boldsymbol{x}_i) \cdot \exp\{v - u\}.$$

Here, $F(\boldsymbol{x}_i)$ is the deterministic frontier and $SF \equiv F(\boldsymbol{x}_i)\exp\{v\}$ is the stochastic frontier proper. The stochastic frontier is a random variable, even conditional on the regressors. For any τ, assuming independence between the error term and the regressors, we have,

$$\begin{aligned}
\tau &= G_{SF|x}(Q_{SF|x}(\tau|\boldsymbol{x}_i)|\boldsymbol{x}_i) \\
&= \Pr(F(\boldsymbol{x}_i)e^{v_i} \leq Q_{SF|x}(\tau|\boldsymbol{x}_i)|\boldsymbol{x}_i) \\
&= \Pr(v_i \leq \ln Q_{SF|x}(\tau|\boldsymbol{x}_i) - \ln F(\boldsymbol{x}_i)|\boldsymbol{x}_i) \\
&= G_{v|x_i}(\ln Q_{SF|x}(\tau|\boldsymbol{x}_i) - \ln F(\boldsymbol{x}_i)|\boldsymbol{x}_i).
\end{aligned}$$

It follows that

$$\begin{aligned}
Q_{v|x}(\tau|\boldsymbol{x}_i) &= G_{v|x}^{-1}(\tau|\boldsymbol{x}_i) \\
&= \ln Q_{SF|x}(\tau|\boldsymbol{x}_i) - \ln F(\boldsymbol{x}_i) \implies Q_{SF|x}(\tau|\boldsymbol{x}_i) \\
&= F(\boldsymbol{x}_i) \cdot e^{q_v(\tau)}.
\end{aligned}$$

Here we write $Q_{v|x}(\tau|\boldsymbol{x}_i) = q_v(\tau)$, because we examine the case where the error term and its components are independent from the regressors. We see that the CQF of the stochastic frontier is just a scaled function of the deterministic frontier, which keeps the latter's central role in SFA.

We close by mentioning that, irrespective of the specific distribution that we will assume for v, it almost always is symmetric around zero. This immediately implies that in SFA the deterministic frontier is assumed to be the median stochastic frontier.[2]

---

[2]In a conventional production function framework, this has been noted and discussed in Goldberger (1968).

3

Basics of Quantile Regression: The Independence Case

For the remainder of this work, we will assume a linear (affine) regression specification, $f(\boldsymbol{x}_i; \boldsymbol{\beta}) = \alpha + \boldsymbol{x}_i'\boldsymbol{\beta}$. We write the constant term separately because it has a special place both in quantile estimation and in SFA.

In this section (and up to and including Section 9) we assume that the error term is independent from the regressors. This implies that $G_{\varepsilon|x} = G_\varepsilon$, and $q_{\varepsilon|x}(\tau\,|\,\boldsymbol{x}_i) = q_\varepsilon(\tau)$, $\forall \boldsymbol{x}_i$. Then we get from Equation (2.2) and the assumed linearity of $f(\boldsymbol{x}_i; \boldsymbol{\beta})$,

$$Q_{y|x}(\tau\,|\,\boldsymbol{x}_i) = (\alpha + q_\varepsilon(\tau)) + \boldsymbol{x}_i'\boldsymbol{\beta}.$$

Writing as is customary, $Q_{y|x}(\tau\,|\,\boldsymbol{x}_i) = \alpha(\tau) + \boldsymbol{x}_i'\boldsymbol{\beta}(\tau)$, we have, between the regression coefficients $(\alpha, \boldsymbol{\beta})$ and the *quantile* coefficients $(\alpha(\tau), \boldsymbol{\beta}(\tau))$, the correspondence

$$\alpha(\tau) = \alpha + q_\varepsilon(\tau), \quad \boldsymbol{\beta}(\tau) = \boldsymbol{\beta}.$$

We note that no assumption was made about the error term having mean zero. We consider the estimation of regression coefficients and distribution parameters, given an i.i.d. sample, in the linear model

$$y_i = \alpha + \boldsymbol{x}_i'\boldsymbol{\beta} + \varepsilon_i, \quad \varepsilon_i = v_i \pm u_i, \; i = 1, \ldots, n$$
$$g_v(v_i) = g_v(-v_i) \implies E[v_i] = 0, \; v \in (-\infty, \infty), \; u_i \geq 0, \; v_i \perp u_i. \tag{3.1}$$

23

This is a standard bare SFM (without specific distributional assumptions) since it assumes that the error term consists of a random component v that has unbounded support and is symmetric around zero and so it has zero-mean, plus (for a cost frontier), or minus (for a production frontier) an independent non-negative random variable u. The model above usually represents the logarithmic transformation of the original relation. Both error components are assumed continuous. The part $\alpha + x_i'\beta$ represents the deterministic frontier and the sign of the composite error ε_i determines whether a firm will be above or below it.

To proceed with quantile regression we define the *quantile error term* as

$$\varepsilon_i(\tau) \equiv y_i - Q_{y|x}(\tau \mid x_i),$$

and combining previous relations and definitions we have that

$$\varepsilon_i(\tau) = \varepsilon_i - q_\varepsilon(\tau).$$

Rather than direct inversion of the conditional distribution function, the conditional quantile can be determined through

$$\rho_\tau(\varepsilon(\tau)) = \varepsilon(\tau) \cdot (\tau - I\{\varepsilon(\tau) < 0\}), \tag{3.2}$$

where the loss function, $\rho_\tau(\varepsilon(\tau))$, is known as the "check" function, because its graph resembles a check mark, see e.g., Koenker (2005, p. 6). $I\{\cdot\}$ is the indicator function.

The Q-estimator, $b(\tau) = (\hat{\alpha}(\tau), \hat{\beta}(\tau))'$, is found by minimizing

$$b(\tau) = \underset{\alpha(\tau), \beta(\tau)}{\operatorname{argmin}} \left\{ C \equiv \sum_{i=1}^{n} \rho_\tau(\varepsilon_i(\tau)) \bigg| \tau \right\}. \tag{3.3}$$

The quantile probability τ is to be chosen a priori by the researcher (a crucial point to be kept in mind), and this is why we wrote the objective function as being conditioned on τ. The most common method to estimate the parameters of the conditional quantile model through minimization of (3.3) is via linear programming (LP). A variety of simplex methods and other LP solvers have been applied to estimate quantiles, all with high degrees of accuracy. Standard gradient-based optimization approaches will fail given the non-differentiable nature of the check function in its argument. Nevertheless, considering the derivatives of the objective function gives theoretical results that are exact asymptotically and almost exact in finite samples.[1] Next we present certain important algebraic and statistical properties of the Q-estimator.[2]

Main Properties of the Q-Estimator

P1. Let $N(\tau)$ and $Z(\tau)$ denote respectively the number of negative and of exactly zero quantile residuals (up to numerical round-up and precision) from the Q-estimator for quantile τ (the "Q-residuals" thereafter). Let K denote the number of regressors (including the constant term), and n the sample size. Then,

$$Z(\tau) = K, \quad \frac{N(\tau)}{n} \leq \tau \leq \frac{N(\tau) + Z(\tau)}{n}. \qquad (3.4)$$

The first result depends on the continuity of the distribution function of the error term. The second, on the existence of a constant term in the regression. We can understand where it comes from if, ignoring the discontinuity of the indicator function, we differentiate the objective function in Equation (3.3) with respect to $\alpha(\tau)$ and set it equal to zero, as we would do with an everywhere differentiable function in order to obtain a stationary point:

$$\frac{\partial C}{\partial \alpha(\tau)} = -\sum_{i=1}^{n}(\tau - I\{y_i - \hat{\alpha}(\tau) - \boldsymbol{x}_i'\hat{\boldsymbol{\beta}}(\tau) < 0\})$$

$$= -n\tau + \sum_{i=1}^{n} I\{\hat{\varepsilon}_i(\tau) < 0\} = 0 \implies \tau = N(\tau)/n.$$

Since the number of zero Q-residuals is always equal to the number of regressors, which is usually small compared to the sample size, we have in practice, looking at the empirical distribution function (EDF)

---

[1] Both Amemiya (1982) and Buchinsky (1998) used this standard approach to optimization in order to derive the properties of the Q-estimator.

[2] Most of the properties presented here are based on results to be found in Koenker and Bassett (1978) and in Koenker (2005), that are still fundamental readings for the theoretical foundations and properties as well as the potential of quantile regression in empirical studies.

of the Q-residuals for the zero-value quantile,

$$\begin{aligned}\text{EDF}_{\hat{\varepsilon}\,|\,\boldsymbol{x}}(0) &= \frac{1}{n}\sum_{i=1}^{n} I\{\hat{\varepsilon}_i(\tau) \leq 0\} \\ &= \frac{N(\tau) + Z(\tau)}{n} \\ &= \widehat{\Pr}(\hat{\varepsilon}_i(\tau) \leq 0) \approx \tau. \end{aligned} \quad (3.5)$$

Now, in the population, it holds by construction that,

$$\Pr(\varepsilon_i(\tau) \leq 0\,|\,\boldsymbol{x}_i) = \Pr(y_i \leq Q_{y\,|\,\boldsymbol{x}}(\tau)\,|\,\boldsymbol{x}_i) = G_{y\,|\,\boldsymbol{x}}(Q_{y\,|\,\boldsymbol{x}}(\tau)) = \tau.$$

Consider the following probability related to the Q-residuals:

$$\begin{aligned}\Pr(\hat{\varepsilon}_i(\tau) \leq 0\,|\,\boldsymbol{x}_i) &= \Pr(y_i - \hat{\alpha}(\tau) - \boldsymbol{x}_i'\hat{\boldsymbol{\beta}}(\tau) \leq 0\,|\,\boldsymbol{x}_i) \\ &= \Pr(y_i \leq \hat{\alpha}(\tau) + \boldsymbol{x}_i'\hat{\boldsymbol{\beta}}(\tau)\,|\,\boldsymbol{x}_i).\end{aligned}$$

If the Q-estimator is consistent for $(\alpha(\tau), \boldsymbol{\beta}(\tau))$, we have

$$\begin{aligned}\Pr(y_i \leq \hat{\alpha}(\tau) + \boldsymbol{x}_i'\hat{\boldsymbol{\beta}}(\tau)\,|\,\boldsymbol{x}_i) &\longrightarrow_p \Pr(y_i \leq Q_{y\,|\,\boldsymbol{x}}(\tau)\,|\,\boldsymbol{x}_i) \\ &= G_{y\,|\,\boldsymbol{x}}(Q_{y\,|\,\boldsymbol{x}}(\tau)) = \tau.\end{aligned}$$

Namely, we obtained that if the Q-estimator is consistent for the quantile coefficients, we will have

$$\Pr(\hat{\varepsilon}_i(\tau) \leq 0\,|\,\boldsymbol{x}_i) \longrightarrow_p \tau. \quad (3.6)$$

Comparing these results we see that Equation (3.6) is nothing less than the identification condition of the Q-estimator, and it is imposed through its sample-analogue, Equation (3.5). It plays the same role in quantile estimation that property $E[X'\varepsilon] = \boldsymbol{0}$ has in OLS estimation (with a zero-mean error term). In OLS estimation $E[X'\varepsilon] = \boldsymbol{0}$ is the moment assumption that represents the consistency of OLS, and we impose it on the estimator as an identification condition, since we have $X'\hat{\varepsilon}_{OLS} = 0$. In quantile estimation, $\text{plim}[Pr(\hat{\varepsilon}_i(\tau) \leq 0\,|\,x_i)] = \tau$ represents the consistency of the Q-estimator, and in an analogous manner with OLS it is imposed on the Q-estimator's residuals: when a constant is present, as OLS forces its residuals to have zero mean and be orthogonal to the regressors, so the Q-estimator forces *its* residuals to equate the empirical probability of their zero-quantile with the chosen τ. Equation (3.5) is part of the mechanics of the Q-estimator and it will hold irrespective of whether the population relation holds, in the same way again that $X'\hat{\varepsilon}_{OLS} = 0$ defines the OLS estimator irrespective of whether $E[X'\varepsilon] = \mathbf{0}$ actually holds. So Equation (3.5) is the *defining property* of the Q-estimator. As with the case of OLS, if the population relation does not hold, it is equivalent to say that the Q-estimator will be inconsistent for the quantile regression coefficients.

In the various fields that quantile regression has been applied, this identification condition, when true at the population level, is harmless as regards the interpretation of the estimation results, since the interest of the research focuses on the slope regression coefficients, and much of the time on just one slope coefficient of a single treatment variable, and also, along the quantiles of the *dependent* variable.

But in SFA the defining property of the Q-estimator is anything but inconsequential, because the *error* quantile of value zero has special importance and is a focal point of the economic model underlying the statistical specification: it is the "probabilistic location" of the deterministic frontier, and we will discuss this in Section 4.

P2. Consider now the derivatives of the objective function, Equation (3.3), with respect to the vector β of the regression coefficients (since here they coincide with the quantile betas), for $k = 1, \ldots, (K-1)$ stochastic regressors. Using a star to denote a probability limit, $z^* = \text{plim}(z)$,

$$\forall k, \quad \frac{\partial C}{\partial \beta_k} = -\sum_{i=1}^{n} x_{ki}(\tau - I\{y_i - \alpha(\tau) - x_i'\beta < 0\})$$

$$= -\tau \sum_{i=1}^{n} x_{ki} + \sum_{i=1}^{n} x_{ki} I\{\hat{\varepsilon}_i(\tau) < 0\} = 0.$$

This implies that

$$\tau \frac{1}{n}\sum_{i=1}^{n} x_{ki} = \frac{N(\tau)}{n}\frac{1}{N(\tau)}\sum_{i=1}^{n} x_{ki} I\{\hat{\varepsilon}_i(\tau) < 0\}$$

$$\Longrightarrow \bar{X}_k = \bar{X}_k\,|_{\hat{\varepsilon}_i(\tau)<0} \longrightarrow_p E[X_k] = E\left[X_k\,|\,\hat{\varepsilon}_i^*(\tau) < 0\right].$$

Note that the asymptotic result does not invoke consistency of the estimator, since it uses conditioning on the probability limit of the Q-residuals, whatever this plim is. Based on the general decomposition of the unconditional expected value, for some variables (y, z),

$$E[y] = \Pr(z < 0) \cdot E[y \mid z < 0] + [1 - \Pr(z < 0)] \cdot E[y \mid z \geq 0],$$

we finally obtain

$$E[X_k] = E[X_k \mid \hat{\varepsilon}_i^*(\tau) < 0] = E[X_k \mid \hat{\varepsilon}_i^*(\tau) \geq 0], \quad \forall k = 1, \ldots, (K-1). \tag{3.7}$$

In words, the Q-estimator equalizes the sub-sample means for each regressor, between the group that includes the observations with negative residuals, and the group that includes the observations with positive residuals, making these equal to the full-sample average value of that regressor.[3] From a statistical point of view, this property reflects the assumption that the error term is (at least) mean-independent from the regressors. In (production) SF terminology (and remembering that the linear specification follows after taking logarithms), the Q-estimator makes the average firm below the deterministic frontier to be the same as the average firm above this frontier, in terms of log-inputs and both to be equal to the overall average firm (always in terms of inputs, not output).

This property aligns well with the concept of a deterministic frontier: being above or below it does not depend on the input-view of the scale of operations, given that we have assumed that the error term is independent from the regressors.

---

[3] A similar tendency can be detected also in OLS estimation but as far as we know it is not part of the properties of the OLS estimator. This feature is more nuanced that the well known feature of the OLS line passing through the sample mean. Here we have for any quantile that the average of any covariate equals the average from the subsample with negative residuals which in turn equals the average from the subsample with positive residuals.

Consistency of the Q-Estimator

As proven in the literature cited previously, we have

P3. $\hat{\alpha}(\tau) \longrightarrow_p \alpha + G_{\varepsilon|x}^{-1}(\tau) = \alpha + q_\varepsilon(\tau), \quad \tau \in (0,1)$.

Compared to the related result for the OLS estimator in the SFM, $\hat{\alpha}_{OLS} \rightarrow_p \alpha + E[\varepsilon]$, we see that the Q-estimator, while not affected by the possible existence of a non-zero mean error term, it includes its own inconsistency term in the estimation of the constant term of the regression. This happens because the Q-estimator is designed to estimate consistently the coefficients of the conditional quantile function, the quantile coefficients, not the regression coefficients.

P4. $\hat{\beta}(\tau) \longrightarrow_p \beta, \quad \tau \in (0,1)$.

The Q-estimator obeys the coefficient correspondence obtained earlier and estimates consistently the unique slope regression coefficients, irrespective of the τ on which we will condition: in all cases the probability limit is the same. This property depends on the assumption of an i.i.d. error term.[4]

Here the conditional quantile functions differ only by a shift reflected in property **P3**, and, outside SFA, the argument that quantile regression provides a "more complete picture of the conditional distribution" becomes relatively weak, since this conditional distribution has nothing else to reveal, as we change quantiles, except this level shift that, moreover, does not depend on the regressors. But in SFA, even this shift, due solely to the error term, is critical for the goals of research because it relates to the composite error term and therefore to the inefficiency component, while the constant term relates to the deterministic frontier. This is another indication that we should examine quantile regression anew, when it comes to application to the SFM. In any case, the robustness advantage of the Q-estimator compared to OLS

---

[4] Beyond consistency, the recent work of Lee *et al.* (2018) documented a second-order bias of the Q-estimator that is larger towards the tails of a density than near the median. The size of this bias appears (in their simulations) to be of relatively small magnitude.

in possibly contaminated finite samples, remains. This hints that we should think about quantile regression and the Q-estimator distinctly.

Full Consistency of the Q-Estimator. The inconsistency term in the estimation of the constant term of the regression, which is the quantile value of the chosen probability level, will be zero only if it is associated with the probability $\Pr(\varepsilon_i \leq 0 \,|\, \boldsymbol{x}_i) \implies q_\varepsilon(\tau) = 0$. We then have:

Lemma 1-I. *When the error term is independent of the regressors, the Q-estimator will be consistent for all the regression parameters if and only if it is computed at* $\tau = \Pr(\varepsilon_i \leq 0 \,|\, \boldsymbol{x}_i)$.

In case that the error term is symmetric around zero, choosing τ to be 0.5, i.e., the median, makes the inconsistency term equal to zero. Since the assumption of an error term symmetric around zero is routinely made outside SFA, this helps explain why "median regression" appears the predominant choice in quantile regression when robustness is a primary concern: the median is the quantile that makes the Q-estimator fully consistent for the regression coefficients, under a zero-mean error symmetry assumption.

Here the distinction, even the "tension" between quantile regression and the Q-estimator is made clear: if we are interested in estimating the regression coefficients, we want to compute the Q-estimator at $\tau : q_\varepsilon(\tau) = 0$. But this is the quantile at which quantile regression provides no more information than conditional-mean estimation.

The Residuals of the Q-Estimator

P5. Combining properties P3 and P4 we have for the residuals of the consistent Q-estimator,

$$\hat{\varepsilon}_i(\tau) = \varepsilon_i - (\hat{\alpha}(\tau) - \alpha) - \boldsymbol{x}_i'(\hat{\boldsymbol{\beta}}(\tau) - \boldsymbol{\beta}) \longrightarrow_p \varepsilon_i - q_\varepsilon(\tau). \qquad (3.8)$$

We have seen this relation in the beginning of this Section, but we stress it again here because it has important implications for SFA, and we state it as a Lemma.

Lemma 2-I. *When the error term is independent of the regressors, the residuals of the consistent Q-estimator are not consistent predictors of the true error term, except if the conditioning* $\tau : q_\varepsilon(\tau) = 0$.

P6. Property P5 implies, assuming that the error moments exist, that

$$\frac{1}{n}\sum_{i=1}^{n}\hat{\varepsilon}_i(\tau) \longrightarrow_p E[\varepsilon_i] - q_\varepsilon(\tau) \implies \hat{\varepsilon}_i(\tau) - \frac{1}{n}\sum_{i=1}^{n}\hat{\varepsilon}_i(\tau) \longrightarrow_p \varepsilon_i - E[\varepsilon_i].$$
(3.9)

The centered quantile residual converges to the true centered error. But then we can consistently estimate the *central* moments of the error term (and hence also its cumulants) using the centered Q-residuals obtained by estimation at *any* τ:

$$\forall \tau \in (0,1), \quad \frac{1}{n}\sum_{i=1}^{n}\left(\hat{\varepsilon}_i(\tau) - \frac{1}{n}\sum_{i=1}^{n}\hat{\varepsilon}_i(\tau)\right)^r \longrightarrow_p E\left[\varepsilon_i - E[\varepsilon_i]\right]^r, \quad r \geq 2.$$
(3.10)

Contrast with the OLS estimator in a SFM, where it is the *raw* residual moments that estimate consistently the central error moments. This property of the Q-residuals allows the construction of a "corrected" Q-estimator, which we will present in Section 7.

For those to whom centering using estimated quantities appears to inject too much estimation inaccuracy in the result, there is another method: run the Q-estimator at different τ, until one finds the τ_0 for which $n^{-1}\sum_{i=1}^{n}\hat{\varepsilon}_i(\tau_0) = 0$. Here we have essentially $E[\varepsilon_i] = q_\varepsilon(\tau_0)$. Then one can use the raw powers of these quantile residuals to obtain the central moments of the error term.

4

Where Quantile Regression and Stochastic Frontier Analysis Clash

The Unidentified Frontier Object

In a production SFM, we arrive at the linear specification typically by postulating a production function $Y_i = F(\boldsymbol{x}_i)e^{\varepsilon_i}$, and then taking natural logarithms. $F(\boldsymbol{x}_i)$ represents the deterministic production frontier, the maximum output given inputs, absent inefficiency and stochastic disturbances.

The cumulative probability that the actual output does not escape the frontier, or the "probabilistic location" of the deterministic frontier, is defined by

$$\begin{aligned}\tau_{DF} &= \Pr\left(Y_i \leq F(\boldsymbol{x}_i) \mid \boldsymbol{x}_i\right) \\ &= \Pr\left(F(\boldsymbol{x}_i) \cdot e^{\varepsilon} \leq F(\boldsymbol{x}_i) \mid \boldsymbol{x}_i\right) \\ &= \Pr\left(e^{\varepsilon} \leq 1 \mid \boldsymbol{x}_i\right) \\ &= \Pr\left(\varepsilon_i \leq 0 \mid \boldsymbol{x}_i\right).\end{aligned} \quad (4.1)$$

For a cost frontier, we have $C_i = C(\boldsymbol{x}_i)e^{\varepsilon_i}$, with $C(\boldsymbol{x}_i)$ being minimum cost given inputs and absent cost inefficiency and stochastic disturbances. Here the probability that actual cost does not escape below the cost frontier is

$$\Pr\left(C_i \geq C(\boldsymbol{x}_i) \mid \boldsymbol{x}_i\right) = 1 - \Pr\left(\varepsilon_i \leq 0 \mid \boldsymbol{x}_i\right).$$

This is a "tail" probability. We deal with quantile (cumulative) probabilities, and it is evident that the quantile probability of a cost frontier is also $\Pr(\varepsilon_i \leq 0 \mid \boldsymbol{x}_i)$. Since $\Pr(\varepsilon_i \leq 0 \mid \boldsymbol{x}_i) = G_{\varepsilon \mid \boldsymbol{x}}(0)$, both production and cost frontiers are located at the zero-quantile of their respective error terms. This has been singled out by Jradi and Ruggiero (2019) and Jradi *et al.* (2019), but they call it confusingly the "optimal" quantile, or, misleadingly, "the quantile of the stochastic frontier", while it is the quantile of the *deterministic* frontier. We can now restate two critical results of Section 3 using SF terminology:

Lemma 1-I-SF (Lemma 1-I for stochastic frontier models): *the Q-estimator is consistent for all the regression coefficients if and only if it is computed at the quantile probability of the deterministic frontier.*

P1-SF (P1 for stochastic frontier models): *the Q-estimator and its residuals always place the deterministic frontier at the quantile probability on which they are conditioned.*

These results have consequences. From Lemma 1-I-SF we learn that we must find a way to estimate the quantile probability of the deterministic frontier, if we are interested in estimating consistently the regression coefficients *including* the constant term (and we are, because we need it to estimate the deterministic frontier). The only information we can obtain on this quantile probability is through the Q-residuals, and from property P1-SF we learn that they offer us nothing more than what we have imposed on them.

So quantile regression alone is not helpful in this matter. We will need to provide additional structure, in the form of distributional assumptions, to be able to accomplish this task. This is a crucial departure from the standard Q-estimator framework, which was conceived as a way to estimate effects at different distribution quantiles without making distributional assumptions.

Moreover, property P1-SF raises additional issues, related now to the interpretational applicability of quantile regression in SFMs. If, by choosing arbitrarily the τ to condition the Q-estimator, we also choose the estimated probabilistic location of the deterministic frontier, we create a totally artificial result: the deterministic frontier is placed where we decide, not where the data tell us. Additionally, even if we locate the deterministic frontier τ_{DF} through a distributional assumption, then, executing the Q-estimator at any other τ, will produce results that co-exist with an a priori false estimate of where the deterministic frontier lies, and consequently with a false proportion of firms that will be placed inside or outside the deterministic frontier by the Q-estimator. In the case that we are examining (independence between error and regressors), estimating at other τ-values will change only the value of the constant term. But even this single estimate is enough to falsify the picture that SFA is interested in.

Another way to see why choosing arbitrarily the quantile probability to execute estimation creates artificial results has been noted by Kumbhakar *et al.* (2020): estimation of the conditional quantile for a specific value of τ imposes an implicit assumption on the relation between the two components v and u of the composite error term. For example, in the Normal-Half Normal production frontier these components are characterized by their scale parameters, σ_v and σ_u. As we will show in Section 5, the following relation exists between $\lambda = \sigma_u/\sigma_v$ and the quantile of the deterministic frontier,

$$\lambda = \tan(\pi(\tau_{DF} - 0.5)).$$

So, if we choose some arbitrary τ to execute the Q-estimator, and then impose the Normal-Half Normal distributional assumption to proceed further, the arbitrarily chosen τ will determine also the estimated λ through the relation above. But λ relates to the relative strength of inefficiency in the sample, so what we are doing is deciding this relative strength *ex ante* and without any link to the data at hand.

In conclusion, we have found that when the error term is independent from the regressors and identically distributed, quantile regression cannot offer us what we are after in SFA without a distributional assumption, and also, that multiple-quantiles estimation, which is a core advantage of quantile regression, is in direct conflict with one important characteristic, namely the probabilistic location of the deterministic frontier and the relation of the observations of the sample to it. This delivers another blow: *multiple-quantiles estimation should not be pursued in SFMs*.[1]

Having painted a picture as grim as possible, we next present applied SFA studies that have used quantile regression and we examine how they handle these conflicts and conceptual hurdles.

Quantile Regression in Applied SFA Studies

Bernini et al. (2004) is perhaps the first paper to apply quantile regression and the Q-estimator in an SFA study (related to the production function of the Italian hotel industry). They write (p. 378), "...describing the maximum output y attainable from a given vector of input x is the same as estimating the technological equation on the observations in the highest percentiles of the conditional distribution of y given x". This is a clear and unambiguous statement, but in reality, it is no more than a self-fulfilling *ad hoc* a priori assertion that most of the firms in the sample will be below the deterministic frontier, or, in other words, that τ_{DF} will be close to the value unity. To see this we translate the statement in our terminology, and it says "if the τ at which we will execute the Q-estimator is close to its highest values (i.e., close to 1.0), say τ^H, then $Q_{y\,|\,x}(\tau^H \,|\, x) \approx f(x_i; \beta)$." But this implies (see Equation (2.2)) that $Q_{\varepsilon\,|\,x}(\tau^H \,|\, x) \approx 0$ which in turn implies that $\tau^H \approx \tau_{DF}$. In other words the authors asserted "if the τ is high, it will be the τ of the deterministic frontier". Why? We have not even touched the data yet, how can we know where the quantile probability of the deterministic frontier lies?

Subsequently, the authors execute the Q-estimator at quantile probabilities $\tau = 0.5, 0.9, 0.975$, arguing that these represent "different

---

[1]There are two consolation prizes here. The first is that we will not have to correct for "empirical quantile crossing". The optimization routine of the Q-estimator does not prevent the slopes from suggesting that two different quantile curves will cross, which cannot arise theoretically (a variety of methods exist to correct quantile estimators in the case of crossing, one of the most popular being reordering, see Chernozhukov et al., 2010). The second is that as we will see in Section 12, when coupled with a distributional assumption, multiple-quantiles estimation can be used as a technical tool towards a specification test for the distributional assumption.

efficiency levels", and they observe that the estimated slope regression coefficients change value, and interpret that as an indication that the (deterministic) frontier changes at different efficiency levels, closing with a mention to "heterogenous[sic] technologies". In other words, they say that on the same sample, by changing the conditioning τ of the Q-estimator we recover *different deterministic frontiers*. But we have shown that either the error term is independent of the regressors and then the beta estimates at any τ have the same probability limit, or that there is dependence between error term and regressors, in which case the estimates from the quantile regression confound the betas that characterize the deterministic frontier with any effects of the regressors coming through the error term; in such a case, they no longer inform us on the deterministic frontier.[2]

Next we find Knox *et al.* (2007), which is a much more elaborate study than the previous one. The authors examined the efficiency of Texas nursing facilities, using a (pooled) panel data set and a production function SFM. When the time comes to implement quantile regression they write "We argue that the top quantiles (percentiles) of the production function are intuitively appealing estimators of the SPF (stochastic production frontier)". The choice of words matters: "intuitively appealing estimators" just invokes the reasonable belief that in a production setting we expect the frontier to be located at a rather high quantile probability. But they talk about the stochastic frontier, even though we have seen that it should be the deterministic frontier. Moreover, they treat the average residual value as a measure of average inefficiency. In the context of maximum likelihood estimation (which they also implement), this is valid to do, since the MLE provides consistent estimates of the regression betas including the constant term. But in the case of quantile regression, we have seen that the estimate of the constant term is inconsistent, except if we have indeed executed

---

[2]Readers may wonder whether there may be a connection here with the group-frontiers model and the meta-frontier approach, that allows for the existence of many deterministic frontiers in the same sample. The answer is 'no', because it would require a different structure of the model to begin with, and without guarantees that the quantile approach could be usefully applied. Still, this is a possibly interesting open field for research.

the Q-estimator at τ_{DF}. It is no surprise that the two magnitudes differ (see their Table 5.1, p. 82), by three and a half percentage points. This is an indication that the chosen quantile probability by the authors to run the Q-estimator, $\tau = 0.9$ is not compatible with the chosen Normal - Half Normal distributional specification that they use for maximum likelihood.

Behr (2010) used quantile regression to examine the efficiency of commercial, savings and cooperative banks in Germany. Behr (2010, p. 572) writes that "To estimate a production frontier, a quantile regression for $\tau = 0.95$ will describe the production process of firms, using firms positioned at the top five percent limit of the conditional production distribution. These firms can be referred to as representing the efficient production frontier or benchmark banks. While the choice of the $\tau = 0.95$ for production and $\tau = 0.05$ for cost functions coincides with the standard choice of significant levels and is also standard in the context of efficiency estimation (see Land *et al.*, 1993, p. 543), some arbitrariness in the choice of τ will ultimately remain." This is the first time that "some arbitrariness in the choice of τ" is acknowledged. Moreover, the reference that the author uses to support his choice is to Land *et al.* (1993). In there, we read "Only a small fraction of the DMUs (say, 5%) will be assumed to perform better. (Any other suitable threshold fraction may be chosen; the figure 5% is used here just to provide a numerical example.)" So it is hardly "standard in the context of efficiency analysis" as Behr claims.

Kaditi and Nitsi (2010) examined farm production efficiency in Greece using 2007 data. As regards the choice of the conditioning quantile, they soften the language a bit more, writing "Some arbitrariness remains in terms of the choice of τ for the estimation of the production frontier... One might conjecture that the higher the number of observations, the higher the quantile τ can be chosen... it seems evident that the analysis should focus on the top quantiles, as these percentiles represent the production frontier in the upper tail of the conditional distribution where 'best-practice' farms are operating." The authors reject statistically the hypothesis that quantile slope coefficients are the same across quantiles (implying some sort of dependence between production inputs and the error term), but they interpret this as indication of the co-existence of many deterministic frontiers, since they write "Having produced a family of production functions, the attention should now be drawn on the particular segment of the conditional distribution that can reflect the production frontier." By examination of the population of firms above $\tau = 0.95$ and $\tau = 0.99$ they use $\tau = 0.975$ as their location of the frontier. Note that the authors try to distinguish between the concepts of a "production function" and of a "production frontier", which without further elaboration is to be rejected since the very start of efficiency analysis is the equivalence of the deterministic production function with the deterministic production frontier. A novel aspect of this study is that they apply a second-stage estimation where individual efficiency scores are regressed on determinants of inefficiency – but here too they use *quantile* regression as the main estimation method. Essentially the authors acknowledged the existence of heteroskedasticity and attempted to account for it with a two-step procedure.[3]

The argument that it is the more efficient firms that operate at the upper tail of the conditional distribution of output seems almost self-evident: for given inputs we look at where the output is higher because this reflects higher efficiency... But this will hold in a model without stochastic noise. In SFA it is not necessarily true, because we have the noise term to deal with: with the error term being $\varepsilon = v - u$ (production frontier), the higher conditional quantiles of the output are associated with higher quantiles of ε, not necessarily with lower quantiles of the inefficiency u. Nevertheless we will show in Section 8 that we can support such anticipation, qualified, in a conditional probabilistic sense, while in Section 9 we will provide further general support for it. But neither of these results dispenses with the need to pin down the probabilistic location of the deterministic frontier.

Perhaps the simplest way that quantile methods have been applied in the SFM is the nonparametric approach of Kumbhakar and Wang (2010), which they term Corrected Mean Absolute Deviation (CMAD). This is similar in spirit to Modified Ordinary Least Squares (MOLS, usually attributed to Greene, 1980), which is a distribution-free

---

[3]The use of quantile regression in such a second step was also undertaken by Chidmi *et al.* (2011), which is commented, together with the (de)merits of the two-step approach in Section 10.

deterministic approach whereby the production frontier, estimated by OLS, is shifted up by the maximum residual to encapsulate all the data. Kumbhakar and Wang (2010) examine the application of median regression ($\tau = 0.5$) instead of OLS.[4] It is natural to expect CMAD and COLS to deliver different estimates of both inefficiency and technology, the reason being that the mean and median are close mostly when the underlying distribution is symmetric. However, in the presence of inefficiency, the prior is that the composite error is asymmetric, thus, differences between mean and median regression should appear. The authors estimate a sample of Indian dairy farms. The slope coefficient estimates are similar between OLS and median regression, but the empirical distribution of the efficiency estimates of MOLS and CMAD are quite different, as their Figure 11.4 shows.

Wang et al. (2014) adopted the terminology "τ-efficiency" and "τ-frontier". They do not discuss what is the economic meaning of these concepts, but in practice they represent nothing more than a frontier and an efficiency measure that is conditional on the τ chosen (in their case, for their nonparametric estimator, but the idea is the same as with the Q-estimator). In fact they clearly state (p. 676) that this "τ-frontier" will coincide with the production function (the actual frontier) "if and only if τ is equal to the probability of non-negative error". This is what we have shown earlier, but the main issue here is what is the meaning, or the usefulness, of these "τ-frontiers" and the corresponding "τ-efficiency" measures, when τ is *not* equal to τ_{DF}. The authors are silent on the matter.

Kumbhakar et al. (2015) examined scale economies, technical change and efficiency in the Norwegian electricity distribution market. Alongside other models and estimation methods, they also applied quantile regression, noting the similarity of results but also that in the quantile regression model they "excluded inefficiency because we are unaware of quantile regressions that incorporate inefficiency." (p. 298, footnote 7). This is an acknowledgment that quantile regression, as with ordinary

---

[4]It should be mentioned that there is a confusion as regards terminology in the literature. In some papers, Kumbhakar and Wang (2010) included, what we call "MOLS" is called "COLS" (Corrected OLS), while elsewhere it is vice-versa. On this matter see Parmeter (2021).

least squares, cannot decompose the error term and extract separately an estimation of inefficiency.

This issue can be seen in the work of Gregg and Rolfe (2016) who attempted to compare a range of quantile regression estimates to a pure SF framework. Their best fitting quantile for their data was $\tau \approx 0.7$ while the quantile regression estimate most similar to the stochastic frontier estimates was $\tau \approx 0.9$. They suggested (p. 46) to calculate individual efficiency by comparing observed output to the estimated quantile, for any given quantile, and, as such, for different values of τ the level of firm level efficiency will change. With our notation this means to run the Q-estimator at different τ values, and for each τ and each observation, compute the ratio

$$\frac{y_i}{Q_{y\mid x}(\tau \mid \boldsymbol{x}_i)} \approx \frac{\alpha + \boldsymbol{x}_i'\boldsymbol{\beta} + \varepsilon_i}{\alpha + \boldsymbol{x}_i'\boldsymbol{\beta} + q_\varepsilon(\tau)}.$$

Since y_i is data, with this metric the "efficiency index" of a firm will monotonically fall as we examine higher quantiles, because higher τ increases $q_\varepsilon(\tau)$. As regards intra-firm comparisons, at each τ, between two firms with the same set of inputs, the firm with the higher realized *composed* error will be deemed more efficient than a firm with lower realization of the composed error. But a higher realization of the composed error does not necessarily mean low inefficiency – it may mean high positive shock v.

Overall, we observe an awkwardness from the part of those researchers that decided to apply quantile regression for efficiency analysis in a stochastic frontier context. The conceptual conflicts and the practical identification issues are recognized but no systematic solutions have been proposed. Such solutions are required in order to have clarity of methods and reliability of results, and this is what we will attempt to provide in Part II.

Thick Frontier Analysis

Before SFA scholars tried their hand with quantile regression, Berger and Humphrey (1991) introduced "thick frontier analysis", which is a method to perform frontier analysis using quantiles but not as discussed up to now. The approach has not been widely adopted but it deserves our attention, being the first attempt at a "quantile-focused" frontier analysis, and also because recently Tsionas (2020b) gave it a new Bayesian boost and upgrade.

The approach was introduced in relation to a cost-frontier study. Berger and Humphrey (1991) examined the banking sector, and ranked the observations (banks) per average cost.[5] They then argued that the banks in the lowest quartile (25%) of this empirical average-cost distribution should be considered as the relatively more efficient banks, while the upper quartile should be treated as containing the less efficient banks.[6] Based on this argument, the authors then estimated separately cost functions (not frontier functions) for these two subsamples, and proceeded with devising various relative metrics. Of course the approach allows for the finding that the two extreme quartiles do not differ much as regards their cost structure (which would mean that inefficiency does not exhibit high dispersion).

A practical problem with the approach is that it requires large samples, since we will eventually discard the middle half of our sample. Another weakness of the method is that it provides an "average" relative comparison of inefficiencies, not individual measures per observation. Nevertheless, as Kumbhakar and Lovell (2000, p. 178) suggested, one can compute a "counterfactual" individual relative metric of inefficiency of the firms in the upper (inefficient) average cost quartile.

While thick frontier analysis requires less specific statistical assumptions, the question is exactly how it is useful. Kumbhakar and Lovell (2000) concluded their presentation by saying that thick frontier analysis "...is likely to be useless to management and of limited value to policy-makers."

We find this conclusion rather narrow. Berger and Humphrey (1991) showed how we can obtain individual metrics for the less efficient firms,

---

[5]For multi-product firms, this requires the application of an "output aggregator index" to obtain a single-valued measure of average cost. An analogous issue arises when one thinks of examining the quantiles of the estimated deterministic frontier, but this time the need is to decide on an "input aggregator index" to arrive at a productivity or "average output" measure.

[6]This is valid if average cost does not depend on the scale of operations, or when the firms are of comparable size as regards their output.

benchmarked on the more efficient firms, which is a tangible metric for managers ("if they can do it, so can we"). Moreover, assessing the dispersion of inefficiency in an industry (which is what thick frontier analysis is all about at its core) is certainly helpful in fine-tuning policies to maximize their effect given limited public resources.

5

Reconciling Quantile Regression with Stochastic Frontier Models

Practical wisdom regarding the quantile location of the deterministic frontier argues for a quantile probability not too many points away from unity for a production model, and not too many points away from zero, for a cost frontier. This reflects the belief that, stochastic disturbances alone cannot make many firms escape the deterministic frontier. But we have seen that the probabilistic location of the deterministic frontier will be imposed on the estimation results by *our* choice of the τ at which we will execute the Q-estimator. Immediately, the underlying theoretical structure imposes restrictions on the choice of this value: it does not look realistic to run a, say, median regression in an SF production study, because it would imply that $\tau_{DF} = 0.50$, while we would be more inclined to expect something like $\tau_{DF} = 0.80$, for which only 20% of firms will be above the deterministic frontier. Nevertheless, this would still be an arbitrary choice (why 0.80 and not 0.85 or 0.90?), that moreover does not lead to the full consistency of the Q-estimator, which depends on being conditioned on the true τ_{DF}. What we *can* do is *estimate the τ_{DF} that will be consistent with a distributional assumption related to the error term*. We present two methods which have appeared in the literature, each tied to a specific set of distributional assumptions.

The Normal-Half Normal Framework

In the Half Normal setting, where the noise component v is Normal and the inefficiency component u is Half Normal, Jradi et al. (2019) provided a simple iterative approach to recover τ_{DF}.

They use the known result[1] that $E[|\varepsilon|] = \sqrt{\frac{2}{\pi}}\sigma$ for $\sigma^2 = \sigma_v^2 + \sigma_u^2$, in order to construct an estimator for τ_{DF}. Pairing this with the mean of the composite error leads to

$$\frac{\pm E[\varepsilon]}{E[|\varepsilon|]} = \frac{\pm\sqrt{\frac{2}{\pi}}\sigma_u}{\sqrt{\frac{2}{\pi}}\sigma} = \frac{\pm\sigma_u}{\sigma},$$

where $\sigma = \sigma_v\sqrt{1+\lambda^2}$ (see for example Fan et al., 1996) which yields, for a production frontier,

$$\frac{-E[\varepsilon]}{E[|\varepsilon|]} = \frac{\lambda}{\sqrt{1+\lambda^2}}, \tag{5.1}$$

where as before, $\lambda = \sigma_u/\sigma_v > 0$. Jradi and Ruggiero (2019) (following the work of Azzalini and Capitanio, 2014) demonstrated that for the Normal-Half Normal distributional pair, the true quantile for the production frontier is

$$\tau_{DF} = 0.5 + \frac{\arctan(\lambda)}{\pi}. \tag{5.2}$$

Note that when $\lambda > 0 \implies \arctan(\lambda) > 0$, and so the quantile probability of the deterministic frontier will necessarily be no smaller than 0.5. This is inherently imposed by the distributional specification.

Equation (5.2) can be inverted to recover λ

$$\lambda = \tan(\pi(\tau_{DF} - 0.5)),$$

which can then be substituted into Equation (5.1):

$$\frac{-E[\varepsilon]}{E[|\varepsilon|]} = \frac{\tan(\pi(\tau_{DF} - 0.5))}{\sqrt{1+\tan^2(\pi(\tau_{DF} - 0.5))}} = \sin(\pi(\tau_{DF} - 0.5)). \tag{5.3}$$

Finally, the quantile consistent with the deterministic frontier can be recovered directly from the first raw moment of the level and the absolute

---
[1] See Proposition 1 in Azzalini (1986) for example.

value of the composite error

$$\tau_{DF} = 0.5 + \frac{\arcsin(-E[\varepsilon]/E[|\varepsilon|])}{\pi}. \tag{5.4}$$

See Zhang et al. (2021) for an application of this approach. Also, Fusco et al. (2022) combine this approach with the method of Frumento and Bottai (2016) where each quantile coefficient $\beta(\tau)$ is expressed and estimated as the inner product of a vector of sub-parameters and of a vector holding non-linear functions of τ.

Equation (5.4) provides a framework to estimate the location of the stochastic frontier, consistent with the Normal-Half Normal distributional framework. Note that we could not use OLS residuals here, since we need an estimate of $E[\varepsilon]$ and by construction $E[\hat{\varepsilon}_{OLS}] = 0$. An iterative approach embedded in the quantile regression framework is what Jradi et al. (2019) proposed.

To explain their algorithm, begin with a set of specific quantiles $\tau_c = 0.5, 0.51, \ldots, 0.99$, say. Estimate the SFM using quantile regression for each τ_c. For each of these quantile regressions, calculate the residuals, $\hat{\varepsilon}(\tau_c)$ and construct $\hat{\tau}_{DF}$ from (5.4). $\hat{\tau}^*$ is the corresponding τ_c such that $\hat{\tau}^* - \tau_c$ is minimized.[2] The theoretical properties of this estimator of τ_{DF} are currently unknown. The finite sample properties of this approach are also unknown as Jradi et al. (2019) did not compare their proposed approach against more common stochastic frontier estimators (like MLE or COLS).

Another issue that may arise in practice is that $\hat{\tau}_{DF}$ may not be unique. Consider the Monte Carlo setup of Kumbhakar et al. (2020) (their Equation 48) with 1,000 observations and $x \sim \mathcal{U}[0.5, 10]$. With $\sigma_v^2 = 1$ and $\sigma_u^2 = 0.1$ we see that plotting $\hat{\tau}_{DF}$ against τ_c (Figure 5.1) can result in multiple crossings. This issue is likely to persist for either small n and/or a low σ_u/σ_v ratio.

For a cost frontier the equivalent expression to Equation (5.2), is

$$\tau_{DF} = 0.5 - \frac{\arctan(\lambda)}{\pi}, \tag{5.5}$$

---

[2] All of the quantiles could be estimated simultaneously as well.

and one can proceed in the same manner as before.[3] We also see that the distributional assumption imposes that the quantile probability associated with the cost frontier cannot be higher than 0.5. This restriction which is analogous to the one obtained for the production frontier above, stems from the assumption that the noise component v in the composite error $\varepsilon = v \pm u$ has its median at zero. We do not consider this restriction as problematic, because, in real-world terms it implies that we do not allow more than half of the firms in the sample to escape the deterministic frontier solely due to noise (being above it for the production frontier case or being below it for the cost frontier case), and this is hardly unrealistic.

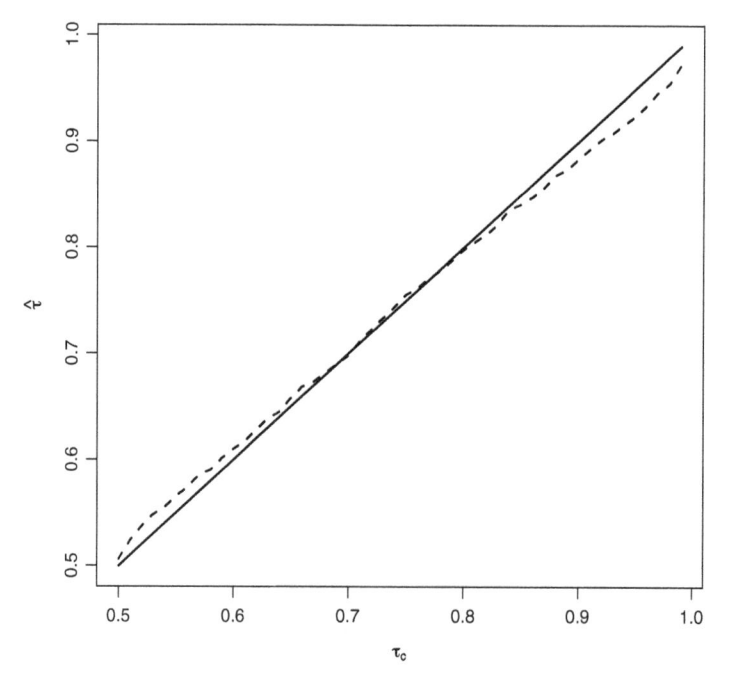

Figure 5.1: Illustration of algorithm of $\widehat{\tau}_{DF}$ of Jradi et al. (2021). Multiple solutions.

---

[3]Related to the iterated algorithm, for a cost model one could select from the set $\tau_c = 0.01, 0.02, \ldots, 0.50$.

The Normal-Exponential Framework

For the Normal-Exponential distributional pair, where the noise component v is Normal and the inefficiency component u is Exponential, Jradi et al. (2021) used a setup like Jradi et al. (2019) to estimate τ_{DF}, that turned out to be similar but simpler, requiring no iterations across quantiles. To explain their approach note that the cumulative distribution function of ε for the Normal-Exponential pair, for the production frontier where $\varepsilon = v - u$, evaluated at $E[\varepsilon] = -E[u] = -\sigma_u$, produces

$$F_\varepsilon(E[\varepsilon]) = F(-\sigma_u) = \exp\left\{\frac{-\sigma_u}{\sigma_u} + \frac{\sigma_v^2}{2\sigma_u^2}\right\} \Phi\left(-\frac{-\sigma_u}{\sigma_v} - \frac{\sigma_v}{\sigma_u}\right)$$
$$+ \Phi\left(\frac{-\sigma_u}{\sigma_v}\right)$$
$$= \exp\left\{-1 + \frac{1}{2\lambda^2}\right\} \Phi\left(\lambda - \lambda^{-1}\right) + \Phi(-\lambda). \quad (5.6)$$

This is useful because it depends on the single parameter λ and because $F_\varepsilon(E[\varepsilon]) \equiv p$ can be consistently estimated either from the OLS residuals, or from the quantile residuals. Specifically, because $\hat{\varepsilon}_{OLS} \to_p \varepsilon - E[\varepsilon]$ we have

$$n^{-1}\sum_{i=1}^n I\{\hat{\varepsilon}_{OLS,i} \leq 0\} \approx n^{-1}\sum_{i=1}^n I\{\varepsilon_i - E[\varepsilon] \leq 0\}$$
$$= n^{-1}\sum_{i=1}^n I\{\varepsilon_i \leq E[\varepsilon]\} \to_p p.$$

Alternatively, from the properties of the Q-estimator we have that, for any conditioning τ, $\hat{\varepsilon}(\tau) \to_p \varepsilon - q_\varepsilon(\tau)$, so for its sample average, we have

$$\overline{\hat{\varepsilon}}(\tau) \equiv n^{-1}\sum_{i=1}^n \hat{\varepsilon}_i(\tau) \to_p E[\varepsilon] - q_\varepsilon(\tau),$$

therefore

$$n^{-1}\sum_{i=1}^n I\left\{\hat{\varepsilon}_i(\tau) \leq \overline{\hat{\varepsilon}}(\tau)\right\} \approx n^{-1}\sum_{i=1}^n I\{\varepsilon_i - q_\varepsilon(\tau) \leq E[\varepsilon] - q_\varepsilon(\tau)\}$$
$$= n^{-1}\sum_{i=1}^n I\{\varepsilon_i \leq E[\varepsilon]\} \longrightarrow_p p.$$

So in both cases the left-hand-side expression provides a consistent $\hat{p}$. An estimator of λ is then found by solving

$$\exp\left\{-1 + \frac{1}{2\hat{\lambda}^2}\right\} \Phi\left(\hat{\lambda} - \hat{\lambda}^{-1}\right) + \Phi\left(-\hat{\lambda}\right) - \hat{p} = 0. \quad (5.7)$$

This is easily undertaken using a unit root solver[4] given that the relationship is monotonic. An unfortunate aspect of this setup is that there are upper and lower bounds on $F_\varepsilon(-\sigma_u)$ (0.5 and 0.368, respectively), which imposes conditions on $\hat{p}$ for an empirical solution to exist.[5]

The whole algorithm has four steps:

(1) "Regress" y on x to find the residuals $\hat{\varepsilon}$. The practitioner can use either OLS or any selected quantile, in which case we obtain $\hat{\varepsilon}_i(\tau)$.

(2) Calculate the percentage of the OLS residuals that are below zero or the percentage of the quantile residuals that are below $\overline{\hat{\varepsilon}}(\tau)$. Call this percentage $\hat{p}$.

(3) Find the root of Equation (5.7) which gives $\hat{\lambda}$.

(4) The quantile probability of the deterministic frontier is estimated as

$$\hat{\tau}_{DF} = \exp\left\{\frac{1}{2\hat{\lambda}^2}\right\} \Phi(-\hat{\lambda}^{-1}) + 0.5.$$

For a cost frontier where $\varepsilon = v + u$ and $E[\varepsilon] = E[u] = \sigma_u$, the algorithm is the same using the expressions

$$F_\varepsilon(\sigma_u) = \Phi(\lambda) - \exp\left\{-1 + \frac{1}{2\lambda^2}\right\} \Phi\left(\lambda - \lambda^{-1}\right), \quad (5.8)$$

$$\hat{\tau}_{DF} = 0.5 - \exp\left\{\frac{1}{2\hat{\lambda}^2}\right\} \Phi(-\hat{\lambda}^{-1}). \quad (5.9)$$

While the theoretical properties of the estimator for τ_{DF} in Jradi et al. (2021) are currently unknown, they did explore the finite sample properties of this estimator compared with both MLE and COLS. Not unexpectedly MLE and COLS performed better in terms of MSE and

---

[4] uniroot() in the R programming language for example.

[5] Zhao (2021) proposes to use this computational approach also for the Normal-Half Normal specification, where these bounds are even tighter.

bias relative to this quantile approach when the model is correctly specified. However, when Cauchy outliers were introduced, the quantile approach performed better at estimating all of the parameters of the SFM: (β, σ_u, σ_v, and τ_{DF}). Again, this reinforces the idea that in the presence of extreme data points, traditional estimation methods are likely to break down. An open issue for future work is to examine the statistical properties of $\hat{\tau}_{DF}$ from the procedures of Jradi *et al.* (2019, 2021).

6

Likelihood-Based Quantile Estimation

Maximum Likelihood Meets Quantile

The standard estimation method in SFMs is maximum likelihood. Maximum likelihood uses neither the objective function that the Q-estimator uses, nor its estimation algorithm. But there exists a specific variant of an Asymmetric Laplace distribution for which one of the distribution parameters coincides with a quantile probability (a "τ"), and where the corresponding density can be seen as a negative monotonic transformation of the "check" function, the objective function of the Q-estimator. The maximum likelihood estimator will of course rely on the convolution of this density with the density of the inefficiency component. But, because the τ parameter appears in only one of the two densities involved, maximizing the convolution with respect to τ is in the same direction of minimizing the check function, which is what the Q-estimator does.[1]

---

[1] Tsionas (2020a) comments that this link provides a "statistical interpretation" of quantile regression.

This Asymmetric Laplace distribution has density (in extended form)

$$f(v) = \begin{cases} \dfrac{\tau_v(1-\tau_v)}{\sigma_v} \exp\left\{-\dfrac{(\tau_v-1)}{\sigma_v}v\right\} & v \leq 0 \\ \dfrac{\tau_v(1-\tau_v)}{\sigma_v} \exp\left\{-\dfrac{\tau_v}{\sigma_v}v\right\} & v > 0, \end{cases} \quad \sigma_v > 0,\ \tau_v \in (0,1).$$

or compactly,

$$f(v) = \dfrac{\tau_v(1-\tau_v)}{\sigma_v} \exp\left\{-\rho_\tau\left(v/\sigma_v\right)\right\}.$$

One can compute that $\Pr(v \leq 0) = \tau_v$. If we set $\tau_v = 1/2$ we obtain the density of the Laplace distribution, the maximization of which leads to the least absolute deviations (LAD) estimator.[2] Horrace and Parmeter (2018) considered this noise distribution but made no mention of quantile estimation of the SFM.

If we use this density to characterize the noise term in the SFA composite error $\varepsilon = v \pm u$, we allow the noise v to exhibit its own skewness (if $\tau_v \neq 0.5$), and moreover we estimate $\Pr(v \leq 0)$ from the data.[3] This is not the same as before, where we assumed a distribution and matched its theoretical moments to the sample moments of the quantile residuals. Here a quantile probability is directly estimated.

Horrace et al. (2021) considered exactly such an SFM where the inefficiency term follows an Exponential distribution. However, having a

---

[2] The Asymmetric Laplace is intimately connected with quantile regression more broadly. Komunjer (2005) proposes quasi-maximum likelihood estimation based on the 'tick-Exponential' family, which is demonstrated to be equivalent to quantile regression when the tick-Exponential family equals the Asymmetric Laplace family. This natural likelihood generalization is an important development in the progression of likelihood estimation in the quantile setting. The work of Bera et al. (2016) has demonstrated that the first order conditions from maximum likelihood using the Asymmetric Laplace distribution is equivalent to the solution stemming from the maximum entropy problem with moment constraints imposed. See also the work of Poiraud-Casanova and Thomas-Agnan (2000) who proved that the shape parameter τ_v is the quantile probability of the location parameter seen as a quantile value, which in the stochastic frontier setting is set equal to zero.

[3] We also note that the use of the Asymmetric Laplace distribution more generally connects with a recent strand of literature on estimation of the SFM where both error terms can be asymmetric (Bonanno et al., 2015; Badunenko and Henderson, 2021; Wei et al., 2021). This has no direct bearing on quantile estimation however.

Table 6.1: Frontiers and quantile partition of the sample for Asymmetric Laplace noise.

Error Components	Output and Frontiers	Probability Mass
$v \leq 0 \leq u$	$Y \leq SF \leq DF$	τ_v
$0 \leq v \leq u$	$Y \leq DF \leq SF$	$\tau_{DF} - \tau_v$
$0 \leq u \leq v$	$DF \leq Y \leq SF$	$1 - \tau_{DF}$

"quantile parameter" does not ensure estimation of the correct location of the deterministic frontier. This is due to the fact that for their distributional specification, $\varepsilon = v - u$, $v \sim \text{AL}(\sigma_v, \tau_v)$, $u \sim \text{Exp}(\sigma_u)$, and $v \perp u$, we get the probability of the deterministic frontier as

$$\tau_{DF} = \Pr(\varepsilon \leq 0) = \frac{\tau_v(\sigma_u + \sigma_v)}{\tau_v \sigma_u + \sigma_v} = \frac{\sigma_u + \sigma_v}{\sigma_u + \sigma_v/\tau_v}. \tag{6.1}$$

Note that because $u \geq 0$ we have $\Pr(v \leq 0 \leq u) = \Pr(v \leq 0)$. So, even though v is jointly realized with u, τ_v, although it does not reflect the position of the deterministic frontier, it does represent the proportion of firms in the sample that are expected to be below the deterministic frontier *irrespective of their degree of inefficiency*, even if inefficiency is zero. This is summarized in the following inequality that can be obtained from Equation (6.1): $\tau_{DF} > \tau_v$. In fact, with τ_v and τ_{DF} available, we have partitioned the sample as in Table 6.1.

We also note that from Equation (6.1) we obtain $\partial \tau_{DF}/\partial \tau_v > 0$, meaning that the higher τ_v is, the higher τ_{DF} will be, for given σ_v and σ_u. The higher the probability that firms will experience a negative shock, the higher the probability that they will find themselves below the deterministic frontier. This shows that the mathematical properties of the specification align well with intuition.

Another interesting aspect of this specification is, as Horrace et al. (2021) showed, that the standard conditional inefficiency measure, $E[u_i | \varepsilon_i]$ is *constant* for $\varepsilon_i > 0$ (for a production frontier). This result essentially states that in the setting where noise is distributed as Laplace or Asymmetric Laplace, the residuals do not provide enough information to rank efficiency for those observations above the deterministic frontier.[4] Horrace et al.'s (2021) finding connects to the early quantile regression literature that treated all firms with positive residuals as fully efficient, providing a more structural link to the treatment of positive residuals as characterizing full efficiency.

An unfortunate feature of the Asymmetric Laplace-Exponential distributional pairing is that the parameters of it are not identifiable (Papadopoulos, 2022a). This stems from the fact that the Asymmetric Laplace can be written as the difference between two Exponential random variables (with different variances). Horrace et al. (2021) circumvented this issue by modeling the variance of the Exponential component as non-iid, dependent upon determinants of inefficiency.

Finally, we note that there is nothing unique in the Laplace family of distributions that allowed Horrace et al. (2021) to bring a quantile parameter to the surface for the MLE to estimate. Wichitaksorn et al. (2014) developed the general methodology to construct such densities, a "generalized class of skewed distributions", where they use a mixture of two densities, and where the mixing coefficient (that regulates skewness) proves to be a quantile probability parameter.

A Bayesian Framework

The Asymmetric Laplace distribution has also been used recently in a Bayesian framework for estimating SFMs.[5] The paper that described the core methodology is Tsionas (2020a). Extensions can be found in Tsionas et al. (2020) who allowed for endogeneity, Bernstein et al. (2021) who proposed leveraging these two earlier papers while using the Bayesian exponentially tilted empirical likelihood (BETEL) approach of Schennach (2005), and Assaf et al. (2020) who developed a dynamic model of production (dynamic as regards an autoregressive scheme for the values of the model parameters).

---

[4]A similar model can be found in Maneejuk and Yamaka (2021) who studied the Asymmetric Laplace-Half Asymmetric Laplace composite error but they did not derive the corresponding inefficiency scores.

[5]The Bayesian approach was introduced in SFA by Van den Broeck et al. (1994).

Here we focus on Tsionas (2020a) in order to understand how the quantile aspect mingles with the Bayesian approach, and what is the essential output of this method. Tsionas (2020a, p. 1178) notes "Roughly, what we want to do is represent a stochastic frontier model in terms of quantiles of the distribution of the dependent variable", and where "parameters, noise and inefficiency differ by quantile."

This being a Bayesian approach, the unknown parameters are given prior distributions, including τ_v (the author uses "q" for it), since the noise distribution is assumed to be Asymmetric Laplace. Also, Tsionas (2020a) assumes that the inefficiency component follows a Half Normal distribution, and is independent of the noise error component. Realizations of inefficiency are generated through a Markov Chain Monte Carlo (MCMC) algorithm. In the end, we obtain posterior distributions for the parameters under estimation, and also a posterior distribution for inefficiency (p. 1181). And, as should be expected, these posterior distributions are inter-dependent: for example, the posterior distribution of the regression coefficients depends on τ_v and the posterior distribution of τ_v depends on the regression coefficients.

But the MCMC algorithm will also give us the *marginal* posterior distribution for τ_v. This allows us to break the inter-dependence, and consider "most likely" or "representative" values for τ_v based on this marginal posterior distribution. Then, by selecting a different value of τ_v, we obtain distributions for the other parameters (e.g., the regression coefficients) and of the inefficiency, that have different quantitative characteristics (like moments), and so different representative values themselves (like the posterior mean, mode or median). It appears that this is what the author meant by "obtaining estimates of parameters and inefficiency that differ by quantile".

There are several issues that must be noted here. First, the quantile parameter τ_v relates to the distribution of the noise component of the composite error term, not of the dependent variable, not even of the dependent variable conditional on the regressors (for this we would need a quantile parameter related to the composite error term, not to the noise component alone).

Second, we have obtained a distribution of the inefficiency conditional on this quantile probability estimation, and the question is: how can we understand a change in the distribution of inefficiency conditional on a characteristic of the distribution of the noise component (the τ_v), *when noise and inefficiency have been assumed independent?* We start by assuming them structurally independent, and we end up with dependence. This dependence was created by us and the Bayesian method we use, and it reflects the fact that *inference on the two* is not independent. This touches on the abstract philosophical roots of the Bayesian approach and the present work is not the place to discuss them. What we can say is that by this method, we can see how the *estimate* on the one will change if we change the *estimate* of the other, by choosing from the latter's posterior distribution a different "representative" value.

Third, "different inefficiency at different quantile probabilities" does not reflect different inefficiency levels that exists *along* different quantiles of the dependent variable or of the error term. They are "what-if" scenarios: "What if the quantile probability of value zero of the error component was, say, $\tau_v = 0.65$? What would be the inefficiency if $\tau_v = 0.7$?" It is *not* the case that the two resulting posterior inefficiency distributions "co-exist" at *different* quantiles of the noise term. The same remark holds for the τ_v-dependent distributions for the regression coefficients and the deterministic frontier that they characterize. It is *not* the case that we have "uncovered" the existence of "many deterministic frontiers" in the same sample. So the assertion "a model where parameters differ by quantile" is subtly but critically misleading: in reality it means "a model where if the quantile that exists in the data *were* different, we would get different parameters". What the Bayesian approach does is to offer a scientifically sound and systematic way to obtain such different values for the parameters. But it does not trace the quantiles of the same conditional distribution.

Part II
What We Can Do

7
The Corrected Q-Estimator

We have seen earlier that the Q-residuals, coming from executing the Q-estimator at any τ, can provide consistent estimates of the central moments of the error. Given a distributional assumption we can obtain the theoretical expressions for the central error moments, and we can then equate them to the central sample moments of the Q-residuals as we do in COLS. In the standard SFM, where the noise component of the composite error is assumed to be zero-mean and symmetric around zero, its 3rd central moment (i.e., its 3rd cumulant) equals the 3rd cumulant of the inefficiency term (plus or minus, depending on whether we are estimating a cost or a production frontier). With a single-parameter distribution for the inefficiency, like the familiar Half Normal and Exponential distributions, or the Generalized Exponential (Papadopoulos, 2021b), this gives us an equation with a single unknown, the parameter of the inefficiency distribution. With this computed, we can then obtain an estimate for the scale parameter of the noise component by using the expression for the variance of the composite error term (i.e., of the 2nd cumulant).

With these parameter estimates in hand, and the distributional assumption, we can compute the probability of the zero quantile which is $\hat{\tau}_{DF}$. If we have a closed-form expression for the distribution function of the error term, this is just a matter of plugging in the parameter estimates and of computing its value at 0, which is indeed the case for the aforementioned inefficiency distributions and a zero-mean Normal noise component independent from inefficiency. We have just constructed the Corrected Q-estimator which is similar in spirit to the method of Corrected OLS, and can work with any distributional specification that possesses moments.

The Normal-Half Normal Specification

Assuming $v \sim N(0, \sigma_v)$, $u \sim HN(\sigma_u)$, and independent, the two scale parameters can be obtained by solving for σ_v and σ_u from the system of cumulant equations

$$\kappa_3(\varepsilon) = \pm\kappa_3(u) = \pm\frac{4-\pi}{\pi}\cdot\left(\sqrt{2/\pi}\right)\sigma_u^3 \approx \frac{1}{n}\sum_{i=1}^n\left(\hat{\varepsilon}_i(\tau) - \frac{1}{n}\sum_{i=1}^n\hat{\varepsilon}_i(\tau)\right)^3,$$

$$\kappa_2(\varepsilon) = \sigma_v^2 + \left(1 - \frac{2}{\pi}\right)\sigma_u^2 \approx \frac{1}{n}\sum_{i=1}^n\left(\hat{\varepsilon}_i(\tau) - \frac{1}{n}\sum_{i=1}^n\hat{\varepsilon}_i(\tau)\right)^2.$$

The sign in the first will be plus if we have a cost frontier, and minus if we have a production frontier. As regards the deterministic frontier, here the composite error term follows a Skew Normal distribution, and its distribution function can be expressed, among other ways, by the correlated bivariate Normal distribution function $\Phi_2(z_1, z_2; \rho)$ (Amsler et al., 2021; Azzalini and Capitanio, 2014). Using the standard reparametrization $\sigma = \sigma_v^2 + \sigma_u^2$, $\lambda = \sigma_u/\sigma_v > 0$, we have,

$$G_\varepsilon(\varepsilon) = 2\Phi_2\left(\varepsilon/\sigma, 0; \frac{(\pm)\lambda}{\sqrt{1+\lambda^2}}\right)$$

$$\implies G_\varepsilon(0) = \hat{\tau}_{DF} = 2\Phi_2\left(0, 0; \frac{(\pm)\hat{\lambda}}{\sqrt{1+\hat{\lambda}^2}}\right).$$

The bivariate standard Normal distribution is radially symmetric around $(0,0)$ and so for generic variables Z_1, Z_2 we have $\Pr(Z_1 \leq 0, Z_2 \leq 0) = \Pr(Z_1 > 0, Z_2 > 0)$, see Nelsen (1993). Then using a well known result of W. F. Sheppard dating back to the 19th century (see David,

1953), we obtain

$$\hat{\tau}_{DF} = 1 - \frac{1}{\pi}\cos^{-1}\left(\frac{(\pm)\hat{\lambda}}{\sqrt{1+\hat{\lambda}^2}}\right). \qquad (7.1)$$

Note that the sign of λ in both expressions will be plus if we have a *production* frontier and minus if we have a cost frontier. Note also that $\partial\hat{\tau}_{DF}/\partial\sigma_u > 0$ for the production frontier and $\partial\hat{\tau}_{DF}/\partial\sigma_u < 0$ for the cost frontier. This says that the stronger the inefficiency the higher (lower) the value of $\hat{\tau}_{DF}$ for a production (cost) frontier. As average inefficiency increases, the probability mass above the production frontier or below the cost frontier reduces: fewer firms manage to escape the frontier due to the random disturbance component v.

The Normal-Exponential Specification

Assuming $v \sim N(0, \sigma_v)$, $u \sim \text{Exp}(\sigma_u)$, and independent, the two scale parameters can be obtained by the equations

$$\frac{1}{n}\sum_{i=1}^{n}\left(\hat{\varepsilon}_i(\tau) - \frac{1}{n}\sum_{i=1}^{n}\hat{\varepsilon}_i(\tau)\right)^3 = \pm 2\sigma_u^3,$$

$$\frac{1}{n}\sum_{i=1}^{n}\left(\hat{\varepsilon}_i(\tau) - \frac{1}{n}\sum_{i=1}^{n}\hat{\varepsilon}_i(\tau)\right)^2 = \sigma_v^2 + \sigma_u^2.$$

As before, the sign in the first will be plus if we have a cost frontier, and minus if we have a production frontier.

The distribution function of the composite error term here, either for a cost or for a production frontier, can be obtained as a limiting case of the two-tier specification, where the composite error term is $\varepsilon = v + w - u$ (Papadopoulos, 2021a), by setting the appropriate scale parameter equal to zero. We get

$$\hat{\tau}_{DF} = G_\varepsilon(0) = \frac{1}{2} \pm \exp\left\{\hat{\sigma}_v^2/2\hat{\sigma}_u^2\right\}\Phi\left(-\hat{\sigma}_v/\hat{\sigma}_u\right). \qquad (7.2)$$

The sign will be plus if we have a production frontier and minus if we have a cost frontier. Inefficiency affects the quantile probability of the deterministic frontier in the same way as in the NHN specification.

The Normal-Generalized Exponential Specification

Here the specification is $v \sim N(0, \sigma_v)$, $u \sim \text{GE}(2, \theta_u, 0)$ and independent from each other. The distribution of the inefficiency component can be seen as a specific incarnation of the Generalized Exponential distribution introduced by Gupta and Kundu (1999), with shape parameter equal to 2, scale parameter equal to θ_u and location parameter equal to zero. It was developed for use in SFMs in Papadopoulos (2021b), as a distribution that has its mode away from zero. It has density

$$g_u(u) = \frac{2}{\theta_u} \exp\{-u/\theta_u\}(1 - \exp\{-u/\theta_u\}), \quad \theta_u > 0, u \geq 0.$$

The two parameters can be obtained by the equations

$$\frac{1}{n}\sum_{i=1}^n \left(\hat{\varepsilon}_i(\tau) - \frac{1}{n}\sum_{i=1}^n \hat{\varepsilon}_i(\tau)\right)^3 = \pm\frac{9}{4}\theta_u^3,$$

$$\frac{1}{n}\sum_{i=1}^n \left(\hat{\varepsilon}_i(\tau) - \frac{1}{n}\sum_{i=1}^n \hat{\varepsilon}_i(\tau)\right)^2 = \sigma_v^2 + \frac{5}{4}\theta_u^2.$$

The sign in the first will be plus if we have a cost frontier and minus if we have a production frontier. For the quantile probability of the deterministic frontier, we get

Production: $\hat{\tau}_{DF} = G_\varepsilon(0) = \frac{1}{2} + 2\exp\left\{\frac{\sigma_v^2}{2\theta_u^2}\right\}\Phi\left(-\frac{\sigma_v}{\theta_u}\right)$

$$-\exp\left\{\frac{2\sigma_v^2}{\theta_u^2}\right\}\Phi\left(-\frac{2\sigma_v}{\theta_u}\right). \quad (7.3)$$

Cost: $\hat{\tau}_{DF} = G_\varepsilon(0) = \frac{1}{2} - 2\exp\left\{\frac{\sigma_v^2}{2\theta_u^2}\right\}\Phi\left(-\frac{\sigma_v}{\theta_u}\right)$

$$+\exp\left\{\frac{2\sigma_v^2}{\theta_u^2}\right\}\Phi\left(-\frac{2\sigma_v}{\theta_u}\right). \quad (7.4)$$

For other specifications we may not have a closed form expression for the distribution function, in which case we can resort to numerical integration of the composite error density by standard methods over $(-\infty, 0)$ to obtain the estimated value of τ_{DF}. Stead et al. (2022a) propose a method to use the empirical distribution function of a suitably corrected residual series in order to pin down τ_{DF}. The benefit of their method is that we do not need to make a full distributional assumption for the noise component of the composed error term. This offers opportunities for inference as well on the noise distribution.

Once we have computed $\hat{\tau}_{DF}$, we should re-run the Q-estimator at this quantile probability, which is the one that makes the Q-estimator fully consistent. But this points towards an iterative procedure, where we take the new estimates and residuals, re-compute $\hat{\tau}_{DF}$ and recalculate the Q-estimator, until the obtained estimates become invariant to further iterations. Under independence, the Q-estimator is consistent for the slope coefficient for any chosen τ, so we expect this iterative method to converge quickly. If it does not it is a diagnostic signal that the independence assumption may not hold. Doing the iterations is also supported by the Monte Carlo experiments of Liu *et al.* (2008) where they found that median regression performs rather badly when the data have an error term skewed due to inefficiency, compared to the 0.80-quantile regression. In general, in a production function model one could start at the 3rd quartile ($\tau = 0.75$) while in a cost-frontier study somewhere near the 1st quartile ($\tau = 0.25$) could serve as the starting point.

This iterative procedure may give the impression that the estimator we propose is essentially the same as the one developed in Jradi *et al.* (2019) for the Normal-Half Normal specification. But this is inaccurate. There the authors do not exploit the consistency property of the centered Q-residuals, which holds irrespective of the conditioning quantile probability chosen for estimation. Instead they run the Q-estimator at a sequence $\{\tau_c\}$ of many such candidate values and they pick that τ_c for which $|\hat{\tau}_{DF}(\tau_c) - \tau_c| = \min$. The iterative search is critical in arriving at the desired estimate, while for the Corrected Q-estimator, the iteration is mostly an optimization of the estimate over finite-sample variability. Compared to what Jradi *et al.* (2021) proposed for the Normal-Exponential setup, the Corrected Q-estimator differs because it uses a method-of-moments approach while they use a distribution function approach.

The Corrected Q-Estimator and COLS

In a SFM with i.i.d. errors, we have seen that the one remaining advantage of the Q-estimator is its robustness to outliers. This is important, but could we make more specific what this robustness implies, compared to the results we would get if we were to use the Corrected OLS estimator?

We offer two approaches that appear worth exploring: First, suppose that we run both COLS and the Corrected Q-estimator. Under the *same* distributional assumptions each will subsequently give us its own estimate for the location of the deterministic frontier τ_{DF}. Chances are, these two estimates will not be the same. Should we always choose the $\hat{\tau}_{DF}$ given by the Corrected Q-estimator, because, in general "it is more robust"? The breakdown point, which is linked to notions of robustness, decays as τ_{DF} moves further away from 0.5 (the median). In frontier analysis, the relevant quantile could be rather extreme, so this naturally draws into question if quantile regression is more robust that traditional SFA.[1] A possible avenue for study would be to develop a formal statistical test that would assess whether their difference is statistically significant (this would be a vector-of-contrasts or Hausman-type of test). Theoretical treatment or simulations could also provide indications as to the finite-sample performance and the relative efficiency of these two approaches for estimating τ_{DF}, under correct distributional specification but also under misspecification: is the Q-estimator "more robust" in this latter case also?

Second would be to implement a comparative examination of these two estimators with regards to the "Type I and Type II failures" that lurk in the shadows of stochastic frontier estimation.[2] The Corrected Q-estimator is vulnerable to both, as is COLS. It is vulnerable to the "wrong skew problem" (or Type I failure), in case this materializes for the Q-residuals: the assumption about the sign of skewness of the composite error term is embedded in the distributional assumptions and the moment equations we will use to obtain estimates for the error

---

[1] For more on robustness in this case see Stead *et al.* (2022b).
[2] See Olson *et al.* (1980) for the initial discussion of these "failures" and Papadopoulos and Parmeter (2021) for a more recent treatment of them.

distribution parameters, so the estimator will become meaningless in cases where the 3rd moment of the Q-residuals have the opposite sign of the one assumed. The Q-estimator is also vulnerable to Type II failure, where the Q-residual sample moments take such values that they lead to a negative estimate for the variance of the symmetric error component.

One more interesting question is the following: these "failures" come about through the properties of the obtained residuals. Will it be the case, that if COLS residuals exhibit the wrong skew problem, so will the Q-residuals? And at *all* conditioning τ values? The same question applies for the occurrence of a Type II failure. Does the Corrected Q-estimator, with its flexibility of being run at different conditioning τ values (while maintaining essential consistency), have an easier path to avoid these failures? At the theoretical level, this would require exploration of the similarities and the differences of quadratic programming against linear programming. Simulations could of course offer insights into the matter.

8

Quantile-Dependent Efficiency

In the previous section we developed the Corrected Q-estimator, whose main advantage against the COLS estimator is its robustness against outliers and, possibly, existent but non-modeled linear conditional heteroskedasticity of the composed error. If to some readers this does not appear very impressive, we proceed in this Section to define proper quantile-dependent measures of efficiency, both at the sample level, but also for individual observations. This, after all, is what one should expect the ultimate value-added to be, from a quantile-based approach.

Quantile-Dependent Efficiency at Sample-Level

Since we have made distributional assumptions, it would be straightforward to compute the marginal quantiles of the assumed distribution functions of the two error components. But this is useful mostly as part of getting to know quantitatively the marginal distribution of the inefficiency component over the sample in more statistical detail. The issue we face here is that the quantiles of the sum/difference of two independent random variables, do not equal the sum/difference of their individual quantiles. For $\varepsilon = v \pm u$, we have $q_\varepsilon(\tau) \neq q_v(\tau) \pm q_u(\tau)$ in general, and very little research exists on this matter (Liu and David,

1989; Watson and Gordon, 1986). So, in the presence of the stochastic disturbance, the marginal quantiles of the inefficiency component cannot be used as a measure of inefficiency at the sample level, even if the two are statistically independent. For example, suppose we have implemented the Asymmetric Laplace distribution for the noise term in a production model, and we have estimated $\tau_v : q_v(\tau_v) = 0$. This does *not* imply that $q_\varepsilon(\tau_v) = -q_u(\tau_v)$.

What we can do is to *condition* also on the noise term v. For theoretical manipulations, we can do that, even if v is unobserved. But if we condition both on the regressor vector $\boldsymbol{x}_i$ and on the noise component v_i we are essentially conditioning on the stochastic frontier, SF_i.

Production Model-Quantile Technical Efficiency

For a production model $Y_i = F(\boldsymbol{x}_i)e^{v_i}e^{-u_i}$, we examine

$$\Pr\left(Y_i \leq Q_{Y|SF}(\tau \mid SF_i) \mid SF_i\right) = \tau$$
$$\implies \Pr\left(SF_i \cdot e^{-u} \leq Q_{Y|SF}(\tau \mid SF_i) \mid SF_i\right) = \tau$$
$$\implies \Pr\left(e^u \geq \frac{SF_i}{Q_{Y|SF}(\tau \mid SF_i)} \mid SF_i\right) = \tau$$
$$\implies \Pr\left(e^u \leq \frac{SF_i}{Q_{Y|SF}(\tau \mid SF_i)} \mid SF_i\right) = 1 - \tau$$
$$\implies \Pr\left(u \leq \ln SF_i - \ln Q_{Y|SF}(\tau \mid SF_i) \mid SF_i\right) = 1 - \tau$$
$$\implies \ln SF_i - \ln Q_{Y|SF}(\tau \mid SF_i) = q_u(1 - \tau).$$

From this we can obtain the sample-level metric

$$TE_q(\tau) \equiv \frac{Q_{Y|SF}(\tau \mid SF_i)}{SF_i} = e^{-q_u(1-\tau)}. \tag{8.1}$$

The left-hand side is the ratio of *maximum at τ (quantile)* output to the stochastic frontier, given the latter. The right-hand-side is computable for a given set of distributional assumptions and the estimates of the distribution parameters of the inefficiency term. This measure is the quantile analogue to the familiar expected value of the technical efficiency index (or Shephard's output distance function)

$$E[TE_i] = E\left[\frac{Y_i}{SF_i}\right] = E\left[\frac{SF_i e^{-u_i}}{SF_i}\right] = E\left[e^{-u_i}\right],$$

which is routinely taken as an average measure of *efficiency* in the sample.[1] For the $TE_q(\tau)$ metric, instead of placing the actual output value in the numerator we put its quantile conditional on the stochastic frontier and obtain an index of *maximum technical efficiency* per quantile probability. Note that, while we started at the observation level, the conditioning eliminated the individuality and gave us a measure for the sample as a whole. Note also that to obtain this index for τ, we must compute the quantile of u at $1-\tau$. The metric $1-TE_q(\tau)$ is the *minimum* inefficiency index at τ, expressed as a proportion of the stochastic frontier output. So we have a ceiling for efficiency and a floor for inefficiency.

Cost Model-Quantile Cost Efficiency

For the cost frontier model $Y_i = C(\boldsymbol{x}_i)e^{v_i}e^{u_i}$, we likewise have

$$\Pr\left(Y_i \leq Q_{Y|SF}(\tau \mid SF_i) \mid SF_i\right) = \tau$$
$$\Longrightarrow \Pr\left(SF_i \cdot e^u \leq Q_{Y|SF}(\tau \mid SF_i) \mid SF_i\right) = \tau$$
$$\Longrightarrow \Pr\left(e^u \leq \frac{Q_{Y|SF}(\tau \mid SF_i)}{SF_i} \mid SF_i\right) = \tau$$
$$\Longrightarrow \frac{Q_{Y|SF}(\tau \mid SF_i)}{SF_i} = e^{q_u(\tau)}.$$

From this we can obtain the quantile analogue of the familiar sample-level cost-efficiency measure $E[CE_i] \equiv E[SF_i/Y_i]$, by setting

$$CE_q(\tau) \equiv \frac{SF_i}{Q_{Y|SF}(\tau \mid SF_i)} = e^{-q_u(\tau)}. \tag{8.2}$$

---

[1] For a recent recapitulation and presentation of this fundamental metric in efficiency analysis see Sickles and Zelenyuk (2019, ch. 1). But there, the acronym TE is used not for Shephard's output distance function but for its reciprocal, the Farrell output-oriented measure of technical efficiency. Also they use the subscript 'i' to denote an input-oriented measure, not as the observation index.

Here we obtain a quantile-dependent *minimum* cost-efficiency index. Although not intuitively interpretable, it has the nice property of ranging in $(0,1)$, and also, the metric $1 - CE_q(\tau)$ gives us the *maximum* percentage of cost-reduction in order to achieve the cost frontier holding output constant. So in the cost frontier model, we have a floor for efficiency and a ceiling for inefficiency, using the quantile approach.

Quantile Efficiency and Distributional Specifications

If the inefficiency term is assumed Half Normal, $u \sim \text{HN}(\sigma_u)$, then $q_u(\tau) = \sigma_u \Phi^{-1}((1+\tau)/2)$, and so

$$\begin{aligned} TE_q(\tau) &= \exp\left\{-\sigma_u \Phi^{-1}\left(\frac{2-\tau}{2}\right)\right\}, \\ CE_q(\tau) &= \exp\left\{-\sigma_u \Phi^{-1}\left(\frac{1+\tau}{2}\right)\right\}. \end{aligned} \quad (8.3)$$

If inefficiency is specified as Exponential, $u \sim \text{Exp}(\sigma_u)$, then $q_u(\tau) = -\sigma_u \ln(1-\tau)$ and

$$TE_q(\tau) = \tau^{\sigma_u}, \quad CE_q(\tau) = (1-\tau)^{\sigma_u}. \quad (8.4)$$

Finally, if inefficiency is assumed Generalized Exponential, $u \sim \text{GE}(2, \theta_u, 0)$ we have $q_u(\tau) = -\theta_u \ln(1-\sqrt{\tau})$ and

$$TE_q(\tau) = \left(1 - \sqrt{1-\tau}\right)^{\theta_u}, \quad CE_q(\tau) = \left(1 - \sqrt{\tau}\right)^{\theta_u}. \quad (8.5)$$

Numerical explorations for common *standard deviations* (*not* common scale parameters), reveal that in both the production and cost frontier models, assuming the Exponential distribution for inefficiency leads to higher estimated efficiency, compared to what we obtain if we assume instead either the Half Normal or Generalized Exponential distributions, over almost all quantile probabilities $\tau \in (0.02, 0.98)$. This result also holds for the traditional expected value efficiency measures $E[TE_i]$ and $E[CE_i]$: the Half Normal is inherently more austere as regards sample-level efficiency compared to the Exponential. The relation between the Half Normal and the Generalized Exponential exhibits more mathematical variety but for the quantile probabilities that matter (high values in the production model, low values in the cost model), the

GE specification gives close but even lower efficiency values than the Half Normal assumption.

Closing this section, one could ask, "once we condition on v also, what difference remains from the DEA/deterministic frontier approach?" Well, conditioning on a random variable does not eliminate this variable from the model. The quantile efficiency measures that we derived are with respect to the *stochastic*, not the deterministic, frontier. From a technical point of view, v is indeed treated as known, and acts as if we had just included it as an additional regressor. But from an interpretational point of view, differences remain. As we move towards the extreme values of τ, inefficiency tends to be eliminated but the decision-making units still have to face the uncertainty embodied in v. Their output tends to the stochastic frontier, which can be above or below the deterministic one.

The $TE_q(\tau)$ quantile technical efficiency metric increases monotonically with τ, and it partly substantiates the intuition that the more efficient firms operate at the high quantiles of the conditional distribution of output, an assertion that we have encountered earlier while surveying the empirical literature. It holds, but modified to be conditional on the noise error component also, and being computed *after* the estimation stage. With a fixed value for the stochastic frontier, we should not describe the phenomenon as "higher output implies lower inefficiency" because it alludes to a causal relation that does not exist, but simply as "lower inefficiency is equivalent to higher output", which is a tautology, since by definition inefficiency is measured as less output. An analogous result holds for the $CE_q(\tau)$ cost efficiency measure: it increases as τ *decreases*, meaning that inefficiency tends to decrease as we get closer to the cost stochastic frontier (which lies below).

Individual Relative Quantile Efficiency

Suppose that, in a production model estimated in logarithms, we compute the standard individual measure of technical efficiency, $E\left[e^{-u_i} \mid \varepsilon_i\right]$. These are best predictors of individual efficiency in a mean-squared-error sense. Computed over all i, we obtain an empirical distribution – and therefore the quantile probability associated with each $E\left[e^{-u_i}\,|\,\varepsilon_i\right]$, each observation, say τ_i.

At the same time we have earlier computed $TE_q(\tau)$ which characterizes efficiency in the output distribution conditional on the stochastic frontier. Then the metric

$$RTE_q(i) \equiv \frac{E\left[e^{-u_i}\,|\,\varepsilon_i\right]}{TE_q(\tau_i)} = \frac{E\left[e^{-u_i}\,|\,\varepsilon_i\right]}{e^{-q_u(1-\tau_i)}}, \qquad (8.6)$$

is meaningful: it gives us the predicted *minimum relative technical efficiency* of decision-making unit i. It is "relative" to the efficiency that characterizes the τ at which this individual observation resides per the individual predicted measure (hence the subscript i in τ), and it is "minimum" because the denominator, $TE_q(\tau_i)$ measures the maximum efficiency at τ_i.

Bias

As Wang and Schmidt (2009, pp. 36–37) have noted, conditional expectations are shrinkage predictors, less variable and having lower variance than what they predict. This means that on average we tend to overestimate e^{-u_i} when it is small, and we tend to underestimate it when it is large. In practice, the empirical support of $E\left[e^{-u_i}\,|\,\varepsilon_i\right]$ is expected to be more narrow than that of a sample of equal size that would have been drawn from e^{-u_i}.[2] Now, Ondrich and Ruggiero (2001) have proved that if the noise component v in the composite error ε has a log-concave density, the conditional expectation is monotonic in ε. This implies that the ranking of observations according to $E\left[e^{-u_i}\,|\,\varepsilon_i\right]$ will differ little from the ranking obtained based on the residual series $\{\widehat{\varepsilon}_i\}$. In Section 9 we prove that this link between ε and u generalizes, and that at higher quantiles of ε we expect low values for u. The end result is that the rankings based on $E\left[e^{-u_i}\,|\,\varepsilon_i\right]$ (and the associated τ_i values as well) do not mislead us as regards the position of an observation in terms of quantile efficiency.

It follows that the denominator in the $RTE_q(i)$ metric is to be trusted as adequately characterizing the true quantile neighborhood

---

[2]The population support is in both cases $(0, 1)$.

of observation i, while, as said, the numerator is expected to have a certain bias. For low values of τ_i this bias is expected to be positive, overestimating individual technical efficiency, while for high values of τ_i it is expected to be negative, underestimating individual technical efficiency. The underdogs get a pass while the stars get humbled, so to speak. Following practical considerations (that are reminiscent of "Thick Frontier Analysis" but in reverse), perhaps the interquantile range [0.25,0.75] is the safest interval to inspect as regards accuracy.

Cost Frontier

In an analogous manner we can compute a maximum relative cost efficiency metric by

$$RCE_q(i) \equiv \frac{E\left[e^{-u_i}\,|\,\varepsilon_i\right]}{CE_q(\tau_i)} = \frac{E\left[e^{-u_i}\,|\,\varepsilon_i\right]}{e^{-q_u(\tau_i)}}. \tag{8.7}$$

It is "maximum" because $CE_q(\tau_i)$ measures minimum cost efficiency. Note that the higher $RCE_q(i)$ is, the *less* relatively cost-efficient firm i is.

Quantiles of the Conditional Distribution of Inefficiency

At present there does not exist an approach that separates inefficiency from noise in a manner similar to Jondrow et al. (1982), in a quantile sense.[3] However, if the density of the composite error term is specified, then we can also obtain the conditional density $g(u_i\,|\,\varepsilon_i)$, and examine its quantiles *per individual*. That is, rather than estimate the mean or mode of the distribution of $u\,|\,\varepsilon$, one could instead estimate the τth quantile. Note that there is no specific link between estimating τ_{DF} and estimating inefficiency based on its conditional distribution, at a quantile probability equal in value to τ_{DF}.

---

[3] Predictors for the individual level utilizing the composite error are traditionally called "JLMS measures" in SFA due to this article, but to push back against the Law of Eponymy of Stigler (1980), we mention that it was Battese and Coelli (1988) that first derived them for the exponentiated variables.

Production Frontier

From standard results we know, for $\varepsilon_i = v_i - u_i$ and given independence, that

$$g_{u|\varepsilon}(u_i \,|\, \varepsilon_i) = \frac{g_v(\varepsilon_i + u_i)g_u(u_i)}{g_\varepsilon(\varepsilon_i)}.$$

In almost all cases we carry estimation at the logarithmic level, but we are interested in measuring efficiency at the original measurement scale. For a production frontier we denote for compactness the efficiency random variable $TE = e^{-u} \equiv k$. Applying a straightforward change-of-variables we obtain the conditional density function of k,

$$g_{k|\varepsilon}(k_i \,|\, \varepsilon_i) = \frac{1}{k_i} \frac{g_v(\varepsilon_i - \ln k_i) g_u(-\ln k_i)}{g_\varepsilon(\varepsilon_i)}, \quad k \in (0,1).$$

Then either by deriving the corresponding conditional distribution function, or by using numerical integration, we can obtain any conditional quantile $q_{k|\varepsilon}(\tau)$, which will satisfy

$$q_{k|\varepsilon}(\tau \,|\, \varepsilon_i): \int_0^{q_{k|\varepsilon}(\tau)} g_{k|\varepsilon}(k \,|\, \varepsilon_i) dk = \tau.$$

In practice we will use estimated parameters and the residuals. Then, we should use the estimates and the quantile residuals series from estimating $\hat{\tau}_{DF}$, because it is then that we have $\hat{\varepsilon}_i(\hat{\tau}_{DF}) \to_p \varepsilon_i$:

$$\hat{q}_{k|\varepsilon}(\tau \,|\, \varepsilon_i): \int_0^{\hat{q}_{k|\varepsilon}(\tau|\varepsilon_i)} g_{k|\varepsilon}(k \,|\, \hat{\varepsilon}_i(\hat{\tau}_{DF})) dk = \tau. \quad (8.8)$$

For every observation i in the sample, we can obtain a series of conditional quantiles of individual efficiency.[4]

The conditional median can be used as an alternative predictor of efficiency at observation level, instead of the familiar conditional expectation $E[u_i \,|\, \varepsilon_i]$, or the conditional mode. Zeebari (2021) proves that the conditional median is also a monotonic function of the conditioning variable ε_i (as is the conditional expected value and the conditional mode), and explores ways to approximate the true quantile probability of u_i based on the empirical quantile probability of ε_i. The prime target

---
[4] If we are interested in examining *in*efficiency, we should consider the variable $k' \equiv 1 - e^{-u}$.

here is not so much each individual measure separately, but the ranking of firms such a measure can provide.

Except for using it as a predictor, another way to exploit the conditional distribution of (in)efficiency is the following: for a common τ value, compute the $\hat{q}_{k\,|\,\varepsilon}(\tau\,|\,\varepsilon_i)$ for each observation i, and form their empirical frequency distribution. This would give us a picture of how efficiency is *distributed* at each distinct quantile probability τ, conditional on ε_i. We implement this in the empirical application of Section 11.

Cost Frontier

In the cost frontier model, even though here too we examine e^{-u} as we saw earlier, there is a twist: if we carry out estimation at the logarithmic scale we have $\varepsilon_i = v_i + u_i$ and so

$$g_{u\,|\,\varepsilon}(u_i\,|\,\varepsilon_i) = \frac{g_v(\varepsilon_i - u_i)g_u(u_i)}{g_\varepsilon(\varepsilon_i)}.$$

For $k \equiv e^{-u}$ we have $u = -\ln(k)$ and so the transformed density ends up different compared to the production model,

$$g_{k\,|\,\varepsilon}(k_i\,|\,\varepsilon_i) = \frac{1}{k_i}\frac{g_v(\varepsilon_i + \ln k_i)g_u(-\ln k_i)}{g_\varepsilon(\varepsilon_i)}, \quad k \in (0,1).$$

Using this, we can proceed as in the production model to obtain individual cost efficiency measures based on quantiles.

9

From the Composite Error Term to Inefficiency: A Fundamental Result

In Section 4 we traced the conceptual awkwardness of those applied SFA studies that had attempted to use quantile regression in the past. One recurring assertion in these studies was that "at the higher quantiles of the conditional distribution of output the more efficient firms operate". This seemed as unsubstantiated comfort, or perhaps a misguided transfer of givens from the DEA framework, because in SFA the quantiles of the distribution of output conditional on the regressors are the quantiles of the composite error term, not of the inefficiency term.

Nevertheless, we showed in Section 8 that we can support this assertion in a conditional sense, if we were to condition also on the noise error component v. Since v is unobserved, this was a theoretical device that allowed us to obtain computable quantile efficiency measures at the sample level.

In this section we show that the assertion holds further weight. Specifically, we examine what we expect inefficiency to be at the extreme quantiles of the composite error term. And we obtain, in more ways than one, that when the magnitude of the composite error term is high (in a production model), or low (in a cost model), we expect that the inefficiency will not be high in a probabilistic, quantile sense. This result does not depend on any specific distributional assumption on the random variables apart from the assumption of intra-error independence and the usual regularity conditions. Below we show this result for the production model, and we leave the examination of the cost model for interested readers.

In principle one could point out that at high output quantiles (conditional on the regressors only), we could also observe high inefficiency but together with high beneficial values of the noise component. While this is correct, we should still carefully make the distinction between the quantiles on the one hand, and the realizations of a random variable, on the other. It is certainly the case that one can observe output high above the deterministic frontier while incorporating high inefficiency together with an even higher positive v value. But this is the "realizations" point of view (of a lucky firm). The quantile approach to efficiency does not represent random realizations but probabilistic boundaries (which are the combined effect of many feasible realizations).

Using from here on in this section uppercase symbols to distinguish random variables from their realizations, with $\mathcal{E} = V - U$, let $\bar{u} > 0$ be some inefficiency level and let $\bar{\varepsilon} > 0$ be some value of $\mathcal{E}$. Note that the two are not linked in any way, they are chosen separately. We provide probabilistic backing to the assertion that "at high conditional quantiles of output, the more efficient firms operate" in two distinct ways.

The *a priori* Point of View

We first examine the situation where we are about to conduct an empirical study, and we contemplate a priori what could happen with inefficiency in our sample. In such a setup we can assess the aforementioned assertion through the examination of the following joint probability:

$$\Pr\left(U > \bar{u}, \mathcal{E} > \bar{\varepsilon}\right),$$

and its derivative with respect to $\bar{\varepsilon}$. If this derivative is negative, then the joint probability reduces in value as we increase $\bar{\varepsilon}$, reflecting the assertion as a probabilistic statement: the higher $\mathcal{E}$ is realized (the higher we are in the quantiles of the distribution of output conditional on the regressors), the lower the probability that the realized inefficiency will exceed any given threshold. By basic laws of probability we have

$$\begin{aligned}\Pr\left(U>\bar{u},\mathcal{E}>\bar{\varepsilon}\right)&=\Pr\left(U>\bar{u},V-U>\bar{\varepsilon}\right)\\&=\Pr\left(U>\bar{u},U\leq V-\bar{\varepsilon}\right)\\&=\Pr\left(\bar{u}\leq U\leq V-\bar{\varepsilon}\right).\end{aligned}$$

For this probability to make sense the random interval involved should have positive length. But this implies that for $V-\bar{\varepsilon} \leq \bar{u} \implies V \leq \bar{\varepsilon} + \bar{u}$, the probability mass will equal zero. So we have the restriction $V \geq \bar{\varepsilon} + \bar{u}$, for positive probability. Given also the assumption that U and V are independent, we can write this probability using integrals and the indicator function as

$$\begin{aligned}\Pr\left(U>\bar{u},\mathcal{E}>\bar{\varepsilon}\right)&=\int_{-\infty}^{\infty}g_v(v)\cdot I\{v>\bar{\varepsilon}+\bar{u}\}\int_{\bar{u}}^{v-\bar{\varepsilon}}g_u(u)dudv\\&=\int_{\bar{\varepsilon}+\bar{u}}^{\infty}g_v(v)\int_{\bar{u}}^{v-\bar{\varepsilon}}g_u(u)dudv\\&=\int_{\bar{\varepsilon}+\bar{u}}^{\infty}g_v(v)\cdot\left[G_u(v-\bar{\varepsilon})-G_u(\bar{u})\right]dv.\end{aligned}$$

We now consider its derivative with respect to $\bar{\varepsilon}$. Differentiating under the integral sign, we have

$$\begin{aligned}\frac{\partial}{\partial\bar{\varepsilon}}\Pr\left(U>\bar{u},\mathcal{E}>\bar{\varepsilon}\right)&=-g_v(\bar{\varepsilon}+\bar{u})\cdot[G_u(\bar{u})-G_u(\bar{u})]\\&\quad-\int_{\bar{\varepsilon}+\bar{u}}^{\infty}g_v(v)\cdot g_u(v-\bar{\varepsilon})dv\\&=0-\int_{\bar{\varepsilon}+\bar{u}}^{\infty}g_v(v)\cdot g_u(v-\bar{\varepsilon})dv<0.\end{aligned}$$

The sign is guaranteed to be negative since the integrand involves two density functions. So, as we look at higher and higher output quantiles conditional on the regressors (i.e., at higher values of $\bar{\varepsilon}$), the probability that the, independently from noise but jointly realized inefficiency, will exceed any given level $\bar{u}$ *reduces*. It is in this probabilistic sense that we can validate the informal assertion that we have found in the empirical literature.

Note that the only assumption we have made (apart from using well-behaved continuous random variables) was that U and V were independent. We do not think that independence can be relaxed without supplementary assumptions. Suppose that U and V are dependent and co-vary towards the same direction. Then intuitively, the probability that a high value of the composite error term may indeed include a high v-realization together with a high u-realization should become not only feasible but tangibly probable.

The Conditional Point of View

Suppose now that we have run an estimation procedure and we have obtained a series of residuals, i.e., estimates of the composite error term. What can we now say about the unobservable inefficiency as higher and higher values of residuals stare at us? In such a situation the proper probability object to examine is the conditional probability

$$\Pr(U > \bar{u} \mid \mathcal{E} = \bar{\varepsilon}) = 1 - \Pr(U \leq \bar{u} \mid \mathcal{E} = \bar{\varepsilon}),$$

and its derivative with respect to $\bar{\varepsilon}$. To support the empirical assertion, we want

$$\frac{\partial \Pr(U > \bar{u} \mid \mathcal{E} = \bar{\varepsilon})}{\partial \bar{\varepsilon}} < 0 \implies -\frac{\partial \Pr(U \leq \bar{u} \mid \mathcal{E} = \bar{\varepsilon})}{\partial \bar{\varepsilon}} < 0$$

$$\implies \frac{\partial \Pr(U \leq \bar{u} \mid \mathcal{E} = \bar{\varepsilon})}{\partial \bar{\varepsilon}} > 0.$$

Using standard probability rules and L'Hospital's rule, we have,

$$\Pr(U \leq \bar{u} \mid \mathcal{E} = \bar{\varepsilon}) = \frac{\frac{\partial}{\partial \bar{\varepsilon}} \Pr(U \leq \bar{u}, \mathcal{E} \leq \bar{\varepsilon})}{\frac{\partial}{\partial \bar{\varepsilon}} \Pr(\mathcal{E} \leq \bar{\varepsilon})} = \frac{\frac{\partial}{\partial \bar{\varepsilon}} \Pr(U \leq \bar{u}, \mathcal{E} \leq \bar{\varepsilon})}{g_{\varepsilon}(\bar{\varepsilon})}.$$

Manipulating the joint probability in the numerator,

$$\Pr(U \leq \bar{u}, \mathcal{E} \leq \bar{\varepsilon}) = \Pr(U \leq \bar{u}, V - U \leq \bar{\varepsilon}) = \Pr(V - \bar{\varepsilon} \leq U \leq \bar{u}).$$

For $V - \bar{\varepsilon} > \bar{u} \implies V > \bar{\varepsilon} + \bar{u}$, this probability will be zero. Also, note that if $V < \bar{\varepsilon}$ the lower limit becomes equivalent to zero, since $U \geq 0$. Using integrals we have then

$$\Pr(V - \bar{\varepsilon} \leq U \leq \bar{u}) = \int_{-\infty}^{\bar{\varepsilon}} g_v(v) \int_{v-\bar{\varepsilon}}^{\bar{u}} g_u(u) du dv$$

$$+ \int_{\bar{\varepsilon}}^{\bar{\varepsilon}+\bar{u}} g_v(v) \int_{v-\bar{\varepsilon}}^{\bar{u}} g_u(u) du dv$$

$$= \int_{-\infty}^{\bar{\varepsilon}} g_v(v) \cdot [G_u(\bar{u}) - G_u(v - \bar{\varepsilon})] dv$$
$$+ \int_{\bar{\varepsilon}}^{\bar{\varepsilon}+\bar{u}} g_v(v) \cdot [G_u(\bar{u}) - G_u(v - \bar{\varepsilon})] dv$$
$$= G_u(\bar{u})G_v(\bar{\varepsilon}) - 0 + G_u(\bar{u}) \cdot [G_u(\bar{\varepsilon} + \bar{u}) - G_v(\bar{\varepsilon})]$$
$$- \int_{\bar{\varepsilon}}^{\bar{\varepsilon}+\bar{u}} g_v(v) \cdot G_u(v - \bar{\varepsilon}) dv.$$

Terms cancel off and we arrive at

$$\Pr(V - \bar{\varepsilon} < U < \bar{u}) = G_u(\bar{u})G_v(\bar{\varepsilon} + \bar{u}) - \int_{\bar{\varepsilon}}^{\bar{\varepsilon}+\bar{u}} g_v(v) \cdot G_u(v - \bar{\varepsilon}) dv.$$

We need first to differentiate this with respect to $\bar{\varepsilon}$, to obtain the numerator in the expression for the conditional probability,

$$\frac{\partial}{\partial \bar{\varepsilon}} \Pr(U \leq \bar{u}, \mathcal{E} \leq \bar{\varepsilon}) = G_u(\bar{u})g_v(\bar{\varepsilon} + \bar{u}) - g_v(\bar{\varepsilon} + \bar{u})G_u(\bar{u}) + g_v(\bar{\varepsilon})G_u(0)$$
$$+ \int_{\bar{\varepsilon}}^{\bar{\varepsilon}+\bar{u}} g_v(v) \cdot g_u(v - \bar{\varepsilon}) dv.$$

The first two terms cancel, while the third is zero, since $U \geq 0 \implies G_u(0) = 0$. So we are left only with the integral at the end. Moving also $\bar{\varepsilon}$ from the limits of integration to the integrand, we want to evaluate the sign of the derivative

$$\frac{\partial}{\partial \bar{\varepsilon}} \Pr(U \leq \bar{u} \,|\, \mathcal{E} = \bar{\varepsilon}) = \frac{\partial}{\partial \bar{\varepsilon}} \left[\frac{1}{g_\varepsilon(\bar{\varepsilon})} \cdot \int_0^{\bar{u}} g_v(v + \bar{\varepsilon}) \cdot g_u(v) dv \right].$$

It suffices to examine the numerator of the right-hand-side (nRHS) which is

$$\text{nRHS} = g_\varepsilon(\bar{\varepsilon}) \cdot \int_0^{\bar{u}} g_v'(v + \bar{\varepsilon}) \cdot g_u(v) dv - g_\varepsilon'(\bar{\varepsilon}) \cdot \int_0^{\bar{u}} g_v(v + \bar{\varepsilon}) \cdot g_u(v) dv.$$

We can house everything under a single integral, and taking common factors we arrive at

$$\text{nRHS} = \int_0^{\bar{u}} g_u(v) g_\varepsilon(\bar{\varepsilon}) g_v(v + \bar{\varepsilon}) \left[\frac{g_v'(v + \bar{\varepsilon})}{g_v(v + \bar{\varepsilon})} - \frac{g_\varepsilon'(\bar{\varepsilon})}{g_\varepsilon(\bar{\varepsilon})} \right] dv.$$

If this expression is positive, we support the assertion that after observing the residuals, we expect that the higher in value they become, the lower is the expected inefficiency.

The product of the three densities is always positive, so what matters is the difference term inside the brackets. Invoking now the standard menu of distributions used in stochastic frontier analysis, V represents the noise component and is usually assumed to be symmetric and ranging over the reals with vanishing density at the extremes, while U is non-negative, also with vanishing density towards the right. Since $\mathcal{E} = V - U$, its distribution (density) will have negative skew, with the long tail to the left and the short tail to the right. We investigate positive values of $\mathcal{E}$ so we are interested in its short tail. Intuitively, the short tail will decay faster than the long tail, and faster than the tail of V, for a common support value. This implies (taking into account that the derivatives of both densities are expected to be negative at the values of $\mathcal{E}$ that interest us),

$$\frac{|g'_v(\bar{\varepsilon})|}{g_v(\bar{\varepsilon})} < \frac{|g'_\varepsilon(\bar{\varepsilon})|}{g_\varepsilon(\bar{\varepsilon})}.$$

In turn, this means that at least the initial terms of the "summation" represented by the "nRHS" integral (near $v = 0$) will be positive, since the term in brackets will also be positive.

For the Normal-Half Normal specification (which leads to a Skew Normal distribution), this can become more formal. Capitanio (2010) has proven that the short tail of the Skew Normal decays faster than the tail of the Normal distribution. With $V \sim N(0, \sigma_v)$ and $U \sim HN(\sigma_u)$, $\lambda = \sigma_u/\sigma_v$, $\sigma = \sqrt{\sigma_v^2 + \sigma_u^2}$, ϕ the standard Normal density and Φ its distribution function, we have

$$g_v(v + \bar{\varepsilon}) = \frac{1}{\sigma_v}\phi\left(\frac{v + \bar{\varepsilon}}{\sigma_v}\right) \implies \frac{g'_v(v + \bar{\varepsilon})}{g_v(v + \bar{\varepsilon})} = -\frac{v + \bar{\varepsilon}}{\sigma_v^2}.$$

For the Skew Normal we have

$$g_\varepsilon(\bar{\varepsilon}) = \frac{2}{\sigma}\phi\left(\frac{\bar{\varepsilon}}{\sigma}\right)\Phi\left(\frac{-\lambda\bar{\varepsilon}}{\sigma}\right),$$

$$g'_\varepsilon(\bar{\varepsilon}) = \frac{2}{\sigma}\phi\left(\frac{\bar{\varepsilon}}{\sigma}\right)\Phi\left(\frac{-\lambda\bar{\varepsilon}}{\sigma}\right)\left(\frac{-\bar{\varepsilon}}{\sigma^2}\right) - \frac{2\lambda}{\sigma\sigma}\phi\left(\frac{\bar{\varepsilon}}{\sigma}\right)\phi\left(\frac{\lambda\bar{\varepsilon}}{\sigma}\right),$$

and so,

$$\frac{g'_\varepsilon(\bar{\varepsilon})}{g_\varepsilon(\bar{\varepsilon})} = -\frac{\bar{\varepsilon}}{\sigma^2} - \frac{\lambda}{\sigma}\frac{\phi(\lambda\bar{\varepsilon}/\sigma)}{\Phi(-\lambda\bar{\varepsilon}/\sigma)}.$$

The ratio of the standard Normal density over its distribution function is the inverse Mill's ratio, which converges *from above* to its argument. So for $\xi > 0$ (a function of $\lambda \bar{\varepsilon}/\sigma$) we can write

$$\frac{g'_\varepsilon(\bar{\varepsilon})}{g_\varepsilon(\bar{\varepsilon})} = -\frac{\bar{\varepsilon}}{\sigma^2} - \frac{\lambda}{\sigma}\left(\frac{\lambda \bar{\varepsilon}}{\sigma} + \xi\right) = -\bar{\varepsilon} \cdot \left(\frac{1 + \sigma_u^2/\sigma_v^2}{\sigma_v^2 + \sigma_u^2}\right) - \frac{\lambda}{\sigma}\xi.$$

Using these results we have for the term whose sign interests us

$$\frac{g'_v(v+\bar{\varepsilon})}{g_v(v+\bar{\varepsilon})} - \frac{g'_\varepsilon(\bar{\varepsilon})}{g_\varepsilon(\bar{\varepsilon})} = -\frac{v+\bar{\varepsilon}}{\sigma_v^2} + \bar{\varepsilon} \cdot \left(\frac{1 + \sigma_u^2/\sigma_v^2}{\sigma_v^2 + \sigma_u^2}\right) + \frac{\lambda}{\sigma}\xi = -\frac{v}{\sigma_v^2} + \frac{\lambda}{\sigma}\xi.$$

This will indeed be positive at the lower end of the "nRHS" integral (where the variable of integration v will be zero), and it will remain positive as long as

$$v \leq \frac{\sigma_v \sigma_u}{\sqrt{\sigma_v^2 + \sigma_u^2}}\xi.$$

Numerical explorations with this distributional pair show that even though eventually, as we increase the upper bound of the nRHS integral the integrand turns negative for a range of values, overall the integral remains positive, which implies, to return to the very beginning, that the conditional probability of $\Pr\left(U > \bar{u} \mid \mathcal{E} = \bar{\varepsilon}\right)$ is a negative function of $\bar{\varepsilon}$. This may not be an equally definite result as the one we obtain in the previous subsection when we examined the joint-probability point of view, but it certainly provides additional support to the intuitive anticipation that firms characterized by a high positive residual are less likely to have high inefficiency in their production.

These results link to and extend earlier results in the literature that have found that, given specific assumptions like log-concavity of the density of the noise component, ranking the observations in a sample based on the conditional expectation of inefficiency $E[u_i \mid \varepsilon_i]$ (Ondrich and Ruggiero, 2001), or using the conditional mode of a certain inefficiency distribution (Papadopoulos, 2021a), is asymptotically equivalent to ranking them using ε_i.

In light of the convolution involved in obtaining the distribution of $\mathcal{E}$, this result may appear counterintuitive. Specifically, with U and V independent, the survival function (i.e., the complementary probabilities related to $\mathcal{E} = V - U$, $U \geq 0$) can be expressed as

$$\Pr(\mathcal{E} \geq \bar{\varepsilon}) \equiv 1 - G_\varepsilon(\bar{\varepsilon}) = \int_{\bar{\varepsilon}}^{\infty} \int_{0}^{\infty} g_v(\varepsilon + u)g_u(u)dud\varepsilon.$$

Here, irrespective of the value of the threshold $\bar{\varepsilon}$, the probability is obtained by averaging over all the values in the support of U, and it is this that makes the obtained result counterintuitive. We can offer the following thought: given that U tends to reduce the value of $\mathcal{E}$, by increasing the value $\bar{\varepsilon}$ we narrow the allowable values for $\mathcal{E}$, leaving only higher and higher values – but this is equivalent to say that we "narrow the potential" of U to allow these higher values of $\mathcal{E}$ to materialize, while U is also of high value.

10

Quantile Estimation and Inference with Dependence

In Section 2 we have demonstrated that for a linear regression specification we have,

$$Q_{y\,|\,x}(\tau\,|\,\boldsymbol{x}_i) = \alpha + \boldsymbol{x}_i'\boldsymbol{\beta} + Q_{\varepsilon\,|\,x}(\tau\,|\,\boldsymbol{x}_i),$$

and mentioned the general consensus that it is in the cases where there is some form of dependence between the error term and the regressors, that quantile regression becomes a truly valuable approach to estimation and inference beyond standard regression. It can also offer a different kind of robustness: If indeed such dependence exists and so we expect different coefficient values at different quantiles, a conditional-mean regression like OLS may show high sensitivity to small changes in the regressor matrix even though no high degree of collinearity exists.[1]

But the existence of dependence is not to be taken lightly. We first show the relation between the conditional quantile function and the conditional expected value. Consider the marginal (unconditional) quantile function of the error term, $Q_\varepsilon(\tau)$. Integrating it over $[0, 1]$ gives

---

[1] For an example where such robustness of quantile regression is put to use, see Papadopoulos (2022b).

us the expected value $E[\varepsilon]$. To show this, write

$$\int_0^1 Q_\varepsilon(\tau)d\tau = \int_0^1 G_\varepsilon^{-1}(\tau)d\tau$$

By the inverse function theorem,

$$\frac{dG_\varepsilon^{-1}(\tau)}{d\tau} = \frac{1}{g_\varepsilon\left(G_\varepsilon^{-1}(\tau)\right)} \implies d\tau = g_\varepsilon\left(G_\varepsilon^{-1}(\tau)\right) \cdot dG_\varepsilon^{-1}(\tau).$$

Making the change of variables for the differential $d\tau$ in the integral we have

$$\int_0^1 Q_\varepsilon(\tau)d\tau = \int_{-\infty}^\infty G_\varepsilon^{-1}(\tau)g_\varepsilon\left(G_\varepsilon^{-1}(\tau)\right)dG_\varepsilon^{-1}(\tau).$$

But $G_\varepsilon^{-1}(\tau) = \varepsilon$, and so,

$$\int_0^1 Q_\varepsilon(\tau)d\tau = \int_{-\infty}^\infty \varepsilon g_\varepsilon(\varepsilon)d\varepsilon = E[\varepsilon].$$

All these manipulations can be done for the CQF of the error term also, since the regressors will be treated as fixed parameters of it. So we have

$$\int_0^1 Q_{\varepsilon\,|\,x}(\tau \mid \boldsymbol{x}_i)d\tau = E[\varepsilon \mid \boldsymbol{x}_i].$$

It should be clear from the above that in general, dependence will create mean-dependence and so possibly endogeneity of regressors and loss of desirable estimator properties. For such cases, quantile regression models have been developed to account for it and maintain the consistency of the Q-estimator (with respect to the regression coefficients), see Wüthrich (2020) for a comparative assessment of the two most-used of these models, instrumental variable quantile regression (IVQR) and local quantile treatment effects (LQTE).

The basic quantile regression model can preserve the consistency of the Q-estimator if dependence between regressors and error term is modeled as conditional heteroskedasticity that enters linearly. Specifically, Koenker and Bassett (1982) have proposed to model a heteroskedastic regression error term as

$$\varepsilon_i = (1 + \boldsymbol{x}_i'\boldsymbol{\gamma})v_i,$$

where v_i is zero-mean, i.i.d and independent from the regressors $\boldsymbol{x}_i$. As the authors note (p. 45) *"this linear scale model of heteroscedasticity is an important special case of the general class of models with linear conditional quantile functions. It subsumes many models of systematic heteroscedasticity which have appeared in the econometrics literature"* – and it nests the homoskedastic case (for $\boldsymbol{\gamma} = \boldsymbol{0}$). So the linear formulation is not as restrictive as it seems. In this model, we have $E[\varepsilon_i \,|\, \boldsymbol{x}_i] = 0 \implies E[\varepsilon_i] = 0$, while the CQF of the dependent variable becomes (generalizing Model 2 of the simulated example in Section 2),

$$\begin{aligned} Q_{y\,|\,x}(\tau\,|\,\boldsymbol{x}_i) &= \alpha + \boldsymbol{x}_i'\boldsymbol{\beta} + (1 + \boldsymbol{x}_i'\boldsymbol{\gamma})q_v(\tau) \\ &= (\alpha + q_v(\tau)) + \boldsymbol{x}_i'(\boldsymbol{\beta} + \boldsymbol{\gamma}q_v(\tau)). \end{aligned}$$

We must remember that the Q-estimator is consistent with respect to the quantile coefficients, not the regression coefficients. If we specify a CQF

$$Q_{y\,|\,x}(\tau\,|\,\boldsymbol{x}_i) = \alpha(\tau) + \boldsymbol{x}_i'\boldsymbol{\beta}(\tau),$$

we see that we will estimate a single quantile-specific marginal effect for each regressor, by adding together the $\boldsymbol{\beta}$ effects coming from the "systematic" part of the regression with those coming through the error term, $\boldsymbol{\gamma}q_v(\tau)$, since we have the correspondence and consistent estimation

$$\widehat{\alpha}(\tau) \longrightarrow_p \alpha + q_v(\tau), \quad \widehat{\boldsymbol{\beta}}(\tau) \longrightarrow_p \boldsymbol{\beta} + \boldsymbol{\gamma}q_v(\tau).$$

As we have already discussed in Section 2, in SFMs we want to keep separate these two effects, because the one (the "betas") relate to the deterministic frontier, while the other effect (through the error term) relates to confounding effects and/or inefficiency, i.e., to the distance from this frontier. Estimating them as one negates the very purpose of SFA. So in this framework of dependence as conditional heteroskedasticity, where quantile regression shows its merits, we have again a fundamental conflict with SFA.

Heteroskedasticity in SFA

A natural way to model conditional heteroskedasticity in maximum likelihood estimation, is to make the parameters of the error distribution functions of the regressors. Because the density of the composite error term is a convolution of two densities and so contains distinct parameters that some relate to the noise error component and some to the inefficiency component, we can in principle postulate different sets of heteroskedasticity determinants for the noise and for the inefficiency.

In practice, what has been implemented in SFA is the so-called "determinants of inefficiency" approach, where we include only variables which help to explain levels of inefficiency across firms, (for an early discussion see Wang and Schmidt, 2002). Technically, the noise error term v in $\varepsilon = v \pm u$ is treated as homoskedastic while u is treated as depending on covariates, through its distribution parameters. And because the distribution of inefficiency is non-negative with non-zero mean, heteroskedasticity also implies mean-dependence for u. But this does not affect consistency of the maximum likelihood estimator, since we are not by-passing this dependence but model it directly in the likelihood function.[2]

The ability to explain variation in inefficiency across firms is alluring. However, it poses challenges for applied research. First, as noted in Wang and Schmidt (2002), if these variables, call them z, are omitted at the time the frontier is estimated (via maximum likelihood or regression), this will most certainly lead to severe issues both for the estimates of the parameters which make up the frontier as well as any estimates of inefficiency which are subsequently calculated. This also holds true in the quantile setting. Chidmi et al. (2011) estimated the SFM using maximum likelihood and then regressed the corresponding JLMS technical inefficiency scores on determinants using quantile regression. This falls under the umbrella of two-step approaches (Parmeter and Kumbhakar, 2014; Wang and Schmidt, 2002) and is advised against in practice.

---

[2]On the other hand, as we have shown in Section 2, if this is what holds in the data, OLS will be inconsistent for the slope regression coefficients, this being the consequence of heteroskedasticity with a non-zero error mean combined.

Another challenging issue when one wants to deploy linear quantile regression to a SFM, is that, in the presence of heteroskedasticity which occurs when determinants of inefficiency are present, the quantiles can no longer be linear in parameters at all quantiles. To make this point clear consider the simple univariate SFM:

$$y_i = \beta_0 + \beta_1 x_i + v_i - u_i, \qquad (10.1)$$

where $v_i \sim N(0, \sigma_v^2)$ and $u_i \sim \sigma(x_i; \delta) u_i^*$ and $u_i^* \sim \mathrm{HN}(1)$ with $\sigma(x_i; \delta) = e^{\delta_0 + \delta_1 x_i}$. For this example we set $\beta_0 = 20$, $\beta_1 = 2$, $\delta_0 = 1$ and $\delta_1 = -0.35$. x_i is a draw from a standard Normal distribution. Figure 10.1 presents the upper and lower deciles of y conditional on x for 1,000 draws from this model. The solid line represents the production frontier while the long dashed lines represent the true decile values and the short dashed lines the estimated linear quantiles. It is clear from the figure that the conditional quantiles are nonlinear, but the degree of nonlinearity changes as τ changes. Moreover, even though $Q_{0.90}(x)$ is nonlinear, the corresponding linear quantile fits it quite accurately; the same cannot be said for $Q_{0.10}(x)$.

That the quantiles are nonlinear is not a probing insight however. As pointed out in Wang and Schmidt (2002), the nonlinearity of the conditional mean stems from the fact that because u is truncated, its conditional mean cannot be linear in parameters, which we discussed earlier. This is also true for the corresponding conditional quantiles. However, what is important to take note of, and to be cognizant of, is that the degree of nonlinearity will differ and this nonlinearity can arise either through v or through u. In the conditional mean setting nonlinearity may arise only through u. This makes proper modeling of the conditional distribution of output all the more important.

The regressors in a SFM (the variables that determine the deterministic frontier) can logically also be predictors of inefficiency. For example, we may want to explore the conjecture that efficiency has an "inverted-U" relationship with the scale of operations: small and large firms tend to be more inefficient than medium sized firms, the small because of lack of know-how, the large because of diminishing returns in control mechanisms and creeping bureaucracy. Then we would want to include as predictors of inefficiency all or some of the regressors also.

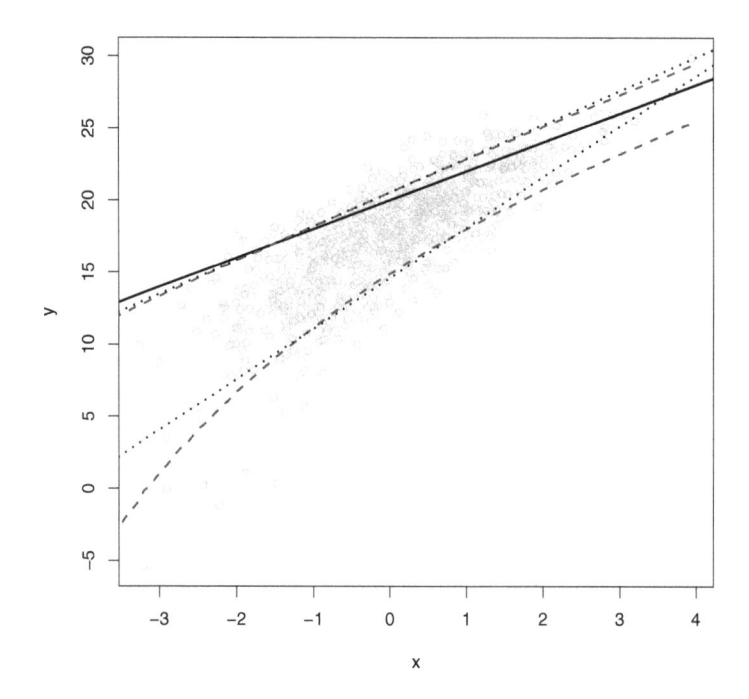

Figure 10.1: Conditional quantile estimation with heteroskedastic u. Simulated data.

The earlier papers that have applied quantile regression to the production frontier setting have not explored determinants of inefficiency. The Q-estimator can be combined with predictors of inefficiency and used in an SFA model without making distributional assumptions, as we show next.

Quantile Regression in a SFM with Predictors of Inefficiency

To model inefficiency in the presence of "determinants of inefficiency" we assume an original relation (say, production) of the form

$$Y_i = F(\boldsymbol{x}_i) \cdot e^{v_i} \cdot [m(\boldsymbol{w}) \cdot \exp\{-h(\boldsymbol{z}_i; \boldsymbol{\delta})\}].$$

Here the last component in brackets is related to inefficiency. $h(\boldsymbol{z}_i; \boldsymbol{\delta}) \geq 0$ is the individual component, with $\boldsymbol{z}_i$ being a vector of available covariates that may overlap with the regressors, and $\boldsymbol{\delta}$ is a vector of constants. On the other hand, $m(\boldsymbol{w}) > 0$ is an average structural efficiency/inefficiency component that is assumed to affect all firms in the sample through the *same* random vector w, and this is why it is not indexed by i. This reflects the fact that, there are market-wide forces to which all firms are subject, like regulations or societal concerns. And with a cross-sectional sample, an econometric study is conducted by implicitly conditioning on them. So w is a random vector, but it is realized the same for all participants, and therefore in the model is treated as fixed, and does not change even when we consider $n \to \infty$ asymptotics, because these asymptotics ask "what would happen if the market got larger", which does not change the conditioning on a given w. Assuming as usual a log-linear DF, taking logarithms we obtain the production SFM

$$y_i = (\alpha + \ln m(w)) + x_i'\beta + v_i - h(z_i; \delta).$$

If this was a cost model, there would be a "plus" sign in front of $h(z_i; \delta)$. We assume that the noise component v_i is independent from (x_i, z_i).

In order to avoid distributional assumptions but also to bring into the model the z-covariates in a usable way, we follow Paul and Shankar (2018) who define $h(z_i; \delta)$ as a deterministic function of the z_i vector, and we make also a functional assumption on u_i:

$$h(z_i; \delta) = \exp\{z_i'\delta\}.$$

The vector δ includes unknown coefficients, and the exponential function guarantees that the expression will always be non-negative.[3] This is reminiscent of the "scaling property" (see e.g., Wang and Schmidt, 2002) but it is not the same, the latter being a full stochastic transformation of a random variable obeying specific characteristics, while we simply assume a functional form for the random individual inefficiency that is convenient for our purposes. With this, the log-regression equation becomes

$$y_i = [(\alpha + \ln m(w)) + x_i'\beta - \exp\{z_i'\delta\}] + v_i.$$

---

[3] Apart from the exponential, one could use other functional forms that guarantee non-negativity.

The reader can now anticipate that we will not be able to identify and estimate separately the inefficiency component $m(w)$ from the regression constant term α. And indeed this is the case. What we did with our formulation was to accept, formalize and rationalize the following recurring technical problem: in principle the vector z should contain an intercept δ_0, however, it is known that separate identification of α and δ_0 can be challenging in small sample settings. Thus, one intercept is commonly suppressed. This in essence does not allow separate identification of both the log-location of the frontier *and* of inefficiency, and it has the following implication: we will not be able to estimate fully the inefficiency component, since $h(z_i; \delta)$ is not the whole story. What the model offers is the focus on the marginal effects of z_i on inefficiency. But this weakness is not specific to the quantile approach, it is an identification issue for any SFM model.[4]

Since what remains as an error term is independent from the regressors, the CQF relation becomes

$$Q_{y\,|\,x,z}(\tau \mid x_i, z_i) = [(\alpha + \ln m(w) + q_v(\tau))] + x_i'\beta \pm \exp\{z_i'\delta\}. \quad (10.2)$$

We have not written out explicitly the conditioning on w, because all cross-sectional studies are implicitly conditioned on it. The consistency of the non-linear Q-estimator has been established by Oberhofer (1982), which applies also here, except for the constant term. For our specific model we have the result:

Lemma 1-D-SF. *In the presence of predictors of inefficiency, that may overlap with the regressors, and assuming that the noise error component is independent of them, all marginal-effects parameters are consistently estimated by non-linear quantile regression at any τ.*

As regards implementation, there exists the package "`quantreg`" in the R statistical platform, curated by many knowledgeable scholars, that can run non-linear quantile estimation.

Property **P1** still holds for the non-linear Q-estimator, because we still include a constant term. Namely, we get, at the chosen τ, $\widehat{\Pr}(\hat{v}(\tau) \leq 0) \approx \tau$. Note that this relates only to the noise component v. Also, properties **P5** and **P6** that relate to the quantile residuals

---

[4] See Parmeter *et al.* (2017) for additional discussion on this.

hold here also. So the central moments of the noise component v are estimated consistently by the quantile residuals centered on their sample mean.

Location of the deterministic frontier. The model cannot determine the quantile probability of the deterministic frontier without further assumptions, because the market-inefficiency index $m(\boldsymbol{w})$ is estimated together with the constant term of the regression.

Measures of inefficiency. The measures developed in Section 8 are inapplicable here, because they all depend on making distributional assumptions, and in the non-linear quantile regression model with determinants of inefficiency, we do not make any, apart from assuming that the noise component v is zero-mean. Moreover, we do not estimate the location of inefficiency. It follows that, in a model with logarithmic dependent variable the empirical mean of the series $\{\exp\{-\exp\{\boldsymbol{z}_i'\hat{\boldsymbol{\delta}}\}\}$ estimates the sample level of *covariate-dependent* technical efficiency, say $E[TE_z]$. Since individual covariate-dependent inefficiency is scaled by the same constant $m(\boldsymbol{w})$, we can still rank the observations per inefficiency by ordering the series. Its empirical density provides a picture as to how this covariate-dependent efficiency is distributed in the sample.

Symmetry tests. We can test whether the noise error component is symmetric, in many different ways, for example by a generalized skewness test as the one proposed in Godfrey and Orme (1991). This is useful because if symmetry is not rejected, we can accept that a *median* regression (at $\tau = 0.5$) will have $q_v(0.5) = 0$. This eliminates one of the terms that are estimated together with the constant term of the regressor.

Wrong skewness problem. Note that the specification imposes a priori an expected skewness sign (by whether we will specify a "plus" or a "minus" in front of $\exp\{\boldsymbol{z}'\boldsymbol{\delta}\}$). If the data point towards the other direction, we conjecture that we will obtain extreme values for the $\boldsymbol{\delta}$ coefficients with such signs so as $\exp\{\boldsymbol{z}'\hat{\boldsymbol{\delta}}\}$ is near zero across observations: since the estimator is not allowed to make this term negative to offset the wrongly specified sign in front of it, it will do the next best thing and make it almost zero. Monte Carlo simulations could investigate this. On the other hand, the non-linear Q-estimator is immune to the Type II failure, since the variance of the v component will be estimated directly from the Q-residuals, without direct connection to other estimated quantities.

Finite sample performance against non-linear least squares. SFMs with predictors of inefficiency can be estimated using the "Scaling property" proper and applying non-linear least squares (NLLS). A useful Monte Carlo exercise would be to compare the finite sample performance of the non-linear Q-estimator at the median against the NLLS estimator. We note that such an undertaking should consider different true distributions for the symmetric error component v: we suggest the Normal, a Student's-t with few degrees of freedom, the Logistic and the Laplace. Also, mixtures of distributions could be considered. The reason for such proposed variety is that the variance of the Q-estimator depends on the true distribution. Moreover, considering different distributions will help us examine the degree to which the robustness of the Q-estimator compared to least-squares actually materializes.

In conclusion, a very different picture emerges when we examine quantile estimation in a SFM with predictors of inefficiency, compared to a model without them: different stochastic assumptions, different estimator, different ways to do inference.

The model we just presented offered a start on quantile estimation of the SFM when determinants are present, but this approach makes two simplifying assumptions. First, the two-sided error is homoskedastic and second, inefficiency is purely deterministic. We have shown that we can make the v-component conditionally heteroskedastic and maintain consistency of the estimator (if we model the heteroskedasticity function as linear in the regressors), but then we will once more estimate together the "direct" effects of the regressors (the beta-coefficients) with those coming through the noise error term.

11

An Empirical Application

To put into empirical context all that we have so far discussed, and for those readers more interested in the application of these methods as opposed to the theoretical underpinnings, we compare the various approaches to estimating the frontier using quantile methods for the timber industry in Norway. Our sample consists of 3,249 farmers for the year 2003 taken from Lien et al. (2007), who use data from the Sample Survey of Agriculture and Forestry, compiled by Statistics Norway in 2004. The data consists of output (measured as annual timber sales), labor (hours worked by the owner, family and hired laborers plus contractors), forest area cut (measured in hectares), and capital (taken as the value of the increment from the forest). For our purposes we will first estimate a simple translog production frontier, specified as

$$\begin{aligned}\ln y_i = {}& \beta_0 + \beta_1 \ln labor_i + \beta_2 \ln area_i + \beta_3 \ln capital_i \\ & + \beta_{11}(\ln labor_i)^2/2 + \beta_{12} \ln labor_i \ln area_i \\ & + \beta_{13} \ln labor_i \ln capital_i + \beta_{22}(\ln area_i)^2/2 \\ & + \beta_{23} \ln area_i \ln capital_i \\ & + \beta_{33}(\ln capital_i)^2/2 + v_i - u_i. \end{aligned} \quad (11.1)$$

Table 11.1: Error component parameter estimates for various quantile estimators of the stochastic production frontier for timber sales.

	COLS			CQ			CDF	
	NHN	NE	NGE	NHN	NE	NGE	NHN	NE
$\hat{\sigma}_v$	0.111	0.144	0.136	0.089	0.137	0.126	0.001	0.110
$\hat{\sigma}_u$	0.250	0.119	–	0.284	0.135	–	0.346	0.157
$\hat{\theta}_u$	–	–	0.115	–	–	0.130	–	–
$\hat{\tau}_{DF}$	0.867	0.736	0.829	0.904	0.760	0.860	0.999	0.810
$\hat{E}[u]$	0.199	0.119	0.173	0.227	0.135	0.195	0.276	0.157
$\hat{E}[TE] = \hat{E}[e^{-u}]$	0.828	0.894	0.848	0.808	0.881	0.831	0.774	0.864
$\hat{SD}(u)$	0.151	0.119	0.129	0.171	0.135	0.145	0.209	0.157

We estimate this model using the Normal-Half Normal setup and method of Jradi *et al.* (2019), the Normal-Exponential setup and method of Jradi *et al.* (2021) (the "CDF" methods), and the Normal-Half Normal, Normal-Exponential and Normal-Generalized Exponential setups described here, using both COLS and the Corrected Q-estimator. Table 11.1 presents the estimates for τ_{DF} and the distributional parameters using these eight different ways.

Several key findings emerge from these results. First, the CDF approach of Jradi *et al.* (2019) under the Normal-Half Normal distributional specification did not converge, the iteration stopped at the upper limit set for τ, which was 0.999. This is surprising given the large sample that we have access to as well as the size of $\lambda = \sigma_u/\sigma_v$, which, via COLS, is larger than 1. Second, we see that the COLS and Corrected-Q estimates for each distributional pair are quite similar, despite one set being estimated using OLS and the other via quantile regression. Third, the CDF approach of Jradi *et al.* (2021) for the Normal-Exponential specification produces a τ_{DF} larger, but similar to those from both the COLS and Corrected Q estimates (0.810 vs. 0.736 and 0.760, respectively).

As regards the measure of efficiency, which due to the logarithmic specification is here the average sample efficiency $E[e^{-u}]$, the results show that indeed the NHN specification is always more pessimistic as

Table 11.2: Estimates of $\hat{\tau}_{DF}$ using iteration with various starting quantiles.

	NHN			NE			NGE		
Starting Quantile	0.5	0.75	0.9	0.5	0.75	0.9	0.5	0.75	0.9
$\hat{\tau}_{DF}$	0.906	0.906	0.906	0.762	0.762	0.762	0.862	0.862	0.862
# Iterations	2	2	2	2	2	2	2	2	2

All estimates obtained using the Corrected Q-estimator.

we have mentioned earlier, while the NGE specification here appears to cut a middle ground between the two benchmark specifications, which is due to the fact that the estimate of the standard deviation of u lies in between the other two.

Returning to our focus on τ_{DF}, we also note that even without iterating the Corrected Q-estimator, the estimates of τ_{DF} were quite compact. Looking at a grid of size 0.001 over 0.5 to 0.99, $\hat{\tau}_{DF}$ ranges from 0.88 to 0.92 for the Normal-Half Normal specification, 0.747 to 0.782 for the Normal-Exponential specification, and 0.844 to 0.875 for the Normal-Generalized Exponential specification. The narrowness of these ranges speaks to the fact that the Corrected Q estimator of τ_{DF} is likely to be impacted relatively little via iteration when ε_i is i.i.d.

To further investigate this we present in Table 11.2 estimates of τ_{DF} using the Corrected Q-estimator and various starting quantiles for each of the three different distributional specifications. Here we use a default tolerance of 0.001. We see immediately for this example that $\hat{\tau}_{DF}$ is not impacted by the choice of starting quantile for the iteration procedure.[1] Further, the estimator in all cases, for all distributional pairs converged in two iterations. The estimated coefficients remained virtually unchanged from iteration to iteration. These features suggest that the Corrected Q-estimator is likely to offer greater empirical tractability over the CDF approaches of Jradi et al. (2019, 2021).

We turn to present now our new quantile-dependent metrics of efficiency. First we tabulate in Table 11.3 the deciles of the sample-level quantile technical efficiency $TE_q(\tau)$ (Equations (8.3) for the NHN, (8.4)

---

[1] We remind the reader that this iterative procedure is fundamentally different from the one required in the CDF methods discussed above.

Table 11.3: Sample-level quantile technical efficiency $TE_q(\tau)$ for different specifications.

τ	NHN	NE	NGE
0.1	0.627	0.733	0.680
0.2	0.695	0.805	0.747
0.3	0.745	0.850	0.790
0.4	0.787	0.884	0.824
0.5	0.826	0.911	0.852
0.6	0.862	0.933	0.878
0.7	0.896	0.953	0.902
0.8	0.931	0.970	0.926
0.9	0.965	0.986	0.952

for the NE and (8.5) for the NGE specifications), using the estimates for the inefficiency distribution parameters per case.

We observe here too the same tendency per specification: the NE specification paints the more positive picture, while the NGE specification moves "in the middle" of the three except for the higher quantiles where it is more conservative than the NHN specification. Recall that these are efficiency *ceilings* per quantile.

Next we present in Figure 11.1 density estimates of the series for *relative* quantile technical efficiency ($RTE_q(i)$ – Equation (8.6)), for the NHN and the NE specifications. We remind the reader that $RTE_q(i)$ measures the technical efficiency of a unit relative to the technical efficiency that characterizes the quantile at which the specific unit resides (i.e., relative to the $TE_q(\tau)$ measure, evaluated at τ_i). Moreover, it is *minimum* relative technical efficiency, a "floor" value. We see that these distributions both have modes near 1 and take values both larger and smaller than 1. This is intuitive as it is well known that depending upon which portion of the distribution one resides in, the technical efficiency estimator shrinks, but the degree of shrinkage will change. $RTE_q(i)$ capture this to some extent. What is interesting is the much greater peakedness of the $RTE_q(i)$ distribution for the Normal-Exponential pair over the Normal-Half Normal pair. The average $E[RTE_q(i)]$ measures are nearly identical across the distributional pairs, 1.042 vs. 1.035 for the Normal-Half Normal and Normal-Exponential, respectively.

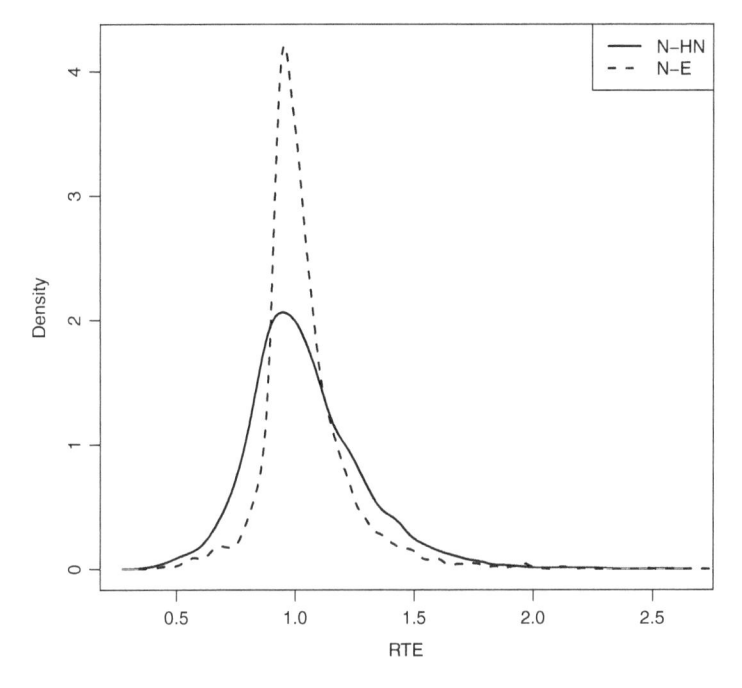

Figure 11.1: Density estimates of relative quantile technical efficiency $RTE_q(i)$ for corrected Q-estimates of normal-half normal and normal-exponential distributional pairs.

Finally, to capture all of the tools we have provided for the empiricist, we plot in Figures 11.2–11.4 the kernel density estimates of the estimated quantile efficiency for each of the three distributional specifications for the Q-estimator for the quartiles (so $\tau = 0.25$, 0.50 and 0.75). Recall that these specific quantile efficiencies are found as in Equation (8.8). What they do is to provide a picture of how individual efficiency scores are distributed around each quantile chosen.

There are several notably features and distinctions from these three plots. First, regardless of the distributional pair, we see that as τ increases from 0.25 to 0.75, the kernel density of the estimated quantile efficiency compresses towards 1. This is intuitive. τ here is capturing the probability of firm level technical efficiency lying below a given quantile. In this case as $\tau \uparrow 1$, the density compresses to 1 as all observations,

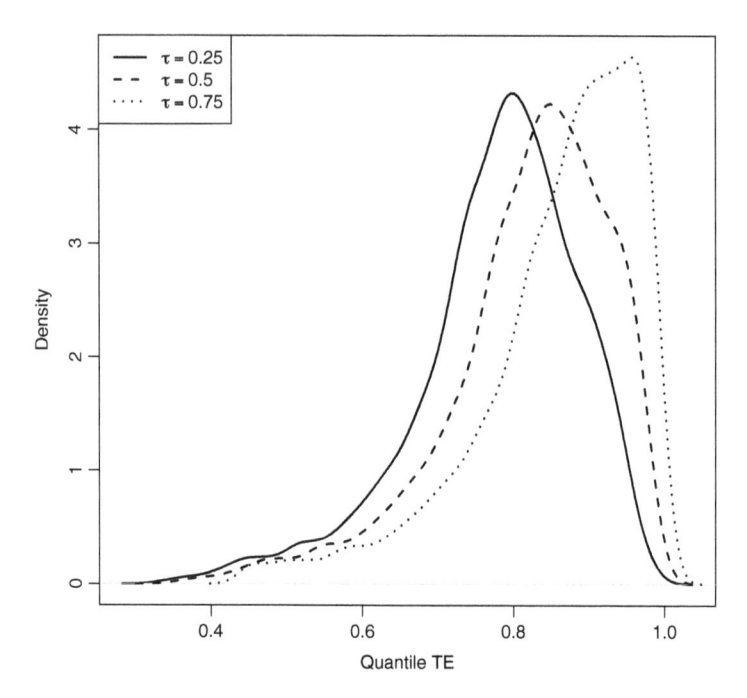

Figure 11.2: Density estimates of individual quantile technical efficiency for corrected Q-estimates of normal-half normal model at the quartiles.

with probability 1, will be below 1. What is interesting is the speed of this compression.

In the Normal-Half Normal setup (Figure 11.2), even for $\tau = 0.75$, there is still considerable variation in the quantile technical efficiency scores. While for the Normal Exponential distributional pair (Figure 11.3) we see a much faster compression towards 1. The Normal-Generalized Exponential (Figure 11.4) is in between the other two setups.

What is a meaningful interpretation of these graphs? Recall that the standard approach with the calculation of efficiency scores is to rely on the mean. This may mislead since the conditional distribution of u given ε is skewed (sometimes heavily so). In this case the mean is not a useful measure of location. Here, reliance on a given quantile presents a more meaningful display of where efficiency is located, based on the users tolerance.

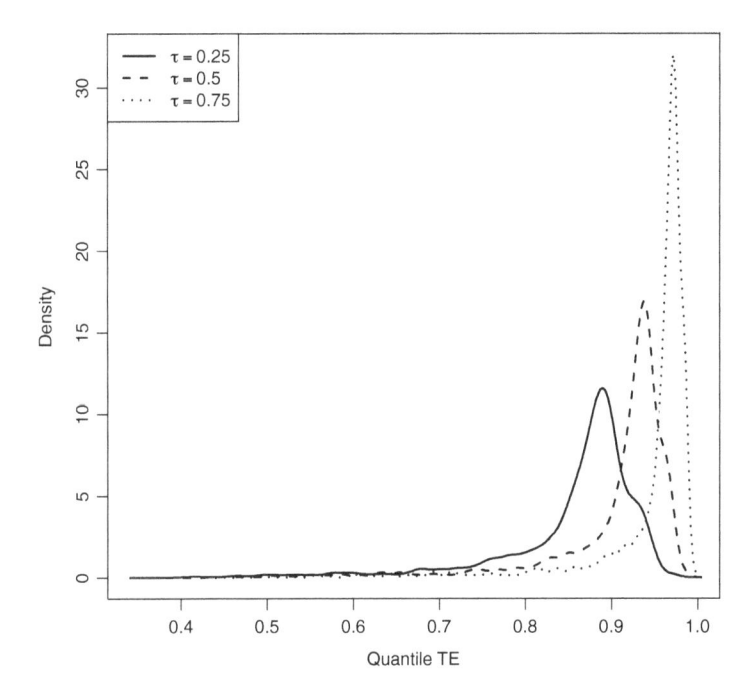

Figure 11.3: Density estimates of individual quantile technical efficiency for corrected Q-estimates of normal-exponential model at the quartiles.

For example, using $\tau = 0.5$, the dashed lines across all three figures inform us as to where half of the efficiency scores lie below. So depending upon how aggressive or conservative a user is, they can select a τ that fits where they wish to assess firm level behavior. This cannot be accomplished using the conditional mean. This use of quantiles paired with the stochastic frontier model is of specific use to consumers of these methods and are easily portable to other distributional settings as well.

Estimation with Determinants of Inefficiency

We also have access to several determinants of inefficiency which we can investigate using the nonlinear Q-estimator discussed in Section 10. These variables are income from recreational services (Z_1), income from agriculture (Z_2), wage income (Z_3), a dummy variable capturing if there

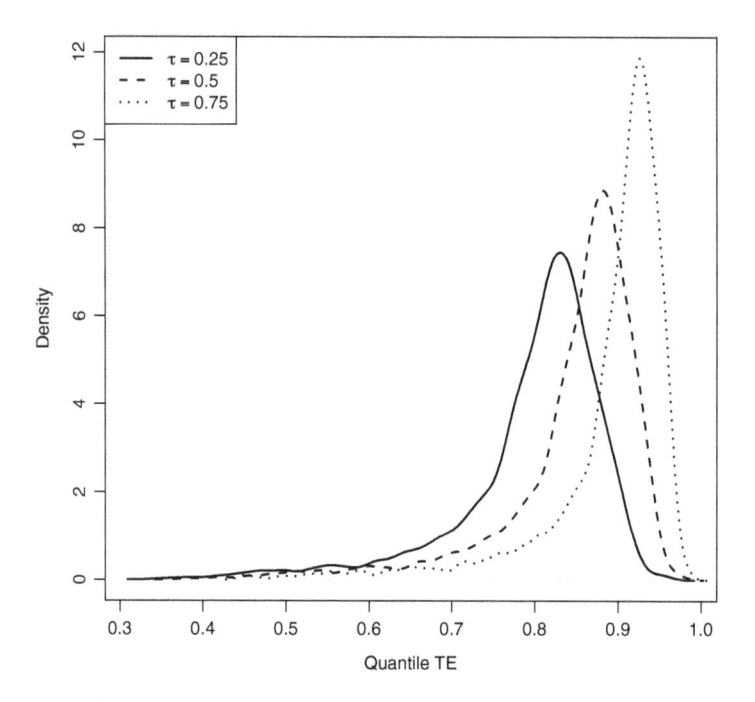

Figure 11.4: Density estimates of individual quantile technical efficiency for corrected Q-estimates of normal-generalized exponential model at the quartiles.

is a management plan in place (Z_4), a dummy variable capturing if the forest owner has a Bachelor's degree or higher (Z_5), and a dummy variable indicating if the properties are located in central municipalities (Z_6). We use the exponential specification for the conditional quantile relation, Equation (10.2), which does not include an intercept in $z_i'\delta$.

In Table 11.4 we present estimates from the nonlinear Q-estimator for various values of τ. Since the remaining error of the model, the noise component v_i is assumed independent of (x_i, z_i), this is a standard technique to informally assess as to whether the independence assumption holds: if the slope coefficient estimates remain relatively stable while the intercept changes, independence is supported.

Several features emerge from Table 11.4. First, as the coefficients of a translog are not clearly interpretable directly, we instead calculate average returns to scale (RTS) for each quantiles to gauge if there are any perceptible differences. We see that from the median up to the

Table 11.4: Estimates of nonlinear quantile stochastic frontier for various quantiles. Standard errors in parentheses.

	$\tau=0.5$	$\tau=0.6$	$\tau=0.7$	$\tau=0.8$	$\tau=0.9$
β_0	3.888	3.860	4.013	4.166	4.676
	(0.140)	(0.191)	(0.346)	(0.506)	(0.538)
β_1	1.076	1.088	1.213	1.234	1.190
	(0.037)	(0.037)	(0.059)	(0.078)	(0.103)
β_2	-0.130	-0.122	-0.162	-0.069	0.087
	(0.035)	(0.034)	(0.059)	(0.087)	(0.123)
β_3	-0.048	-0.046	-0.109	-0.142	-0.217
	(0.025)	(0.037)	(0.065)	(0.093)	(0.097)
β_{11}	-0.018	-0.016	-0.019	-0.029	-0.046
	(0.006)	(0.004)	(0.005)	(0.006)	(0.009)
β_{22}	-0.009	-0.009	-0.019	-0.021	-0.021
	(0.005)	(0.005)	(0.006)	(0.008)	(0.016)
β_{33}	0.007	0.007	0.016	0.020	0.027
	(0.002)	(0.004)	(0.006)	(0.009)	(0.009)
β_{12}	0.013	0.014	0.020	0.027	0.032
	(0.005)	(0.004)	(0.004)	(0.005)	(0.009)
β_{13}	-0.005	-0.006	-0.018	-0.018	-0.012
	(0.003)	(0.003)	(0.006)	(0.007)	(0.010)
β_{23}	0.011	0.011	0.014	0.006	-0.008
	(0.003)	(0.003)	(0.005)	(0.008)	(0.010)
RTS	0.986	1.011	1.001	1.014	0.978
δ_1	0.129	0.186	0.229	0.160	0.130
	(0.090)	(0.123)	(0.145)	(0.174)	(0.150)
δ_2	-0.024	-0.031	-0.042	-0.080	-0.294
	(0.015)	(0.035)	(0.063)	(0.159)	(0.131)
δ_3	-0.003	-0.010	-0.008	-0.003	-0.062
	(0.006)	(0.010)	(0.020)	(0.040)	(0.063)
δ_4	-0.002	-0.003	-0.016	-0.032	-0.024
	(0.001)	(0.003)	(0.006)	(0.009)	(0.016)
δ_5	-0.002	-0.008	-0.016	-0.029	-0.005
	(0.002)	(0.005)	(0.008)	(0.013)	(0.014)
δ_6	0.000	-0.001	-0.002	0.004	0.003
	(0.001)	(0.002)	(0.004)	(0.008)	(0.010)

upper decile average RTS is remarkably stable and very near 1. We also find symmetry of the residuals from median regression across a range of statistical tests.

We also see that the raw coefficient estimates that are inside the exponential function display fairly stable behavior across the quantiles as well. Further, many of the estimated elements of the $\boldsymbol{\delta}$ vector are not statistically significant across the quantiles, only for a given quantile. In general, the independence assumption is supported.

To more reliably understand the impact that any of these six variables have on quantile inefficiency, we calculate their *average* marginal effects on inefficiency. These are computed, for each continuous z_k variable in $\boldsymbol{z}$, as

$$E\left[\frac{\partial \exp\{\boldsymbol{z}'\boldsymbol{\delta}(\tau)\}}{\partial z_k}\right] \approx \hat{\delta}_k(\tau) \cdot \frac{1}{n}\sum_{i=1}^n \exp\{\boldsymbol{z}_i'\widehat{\boldsymbol{\delta}}(\tau)\}.$$

For a binary variable the formula is different. Write Δ for the difference operator, and consider $z_{ik} \in \{0,1\}$. Then, for observation i, the "marginal" effect is

$$\frac{\Delta_{z_k} \exp\{\boldsymbol{z}_i'\boldsymbol{\delta}(\tau)\}}{\Delta z_k} = \left[\exp\{\boldsymbol{z}_i'\boldsymbol{\delta}(\tau)\}\right]_{z_{ik}=1} - \left[\exp\{\boldsymbol{z}_i'\boldsymbol{\delta}(\tau)\}\right]_{z_{ik}=0}.$$

Using a tilde to denote the $\boldsymbol{z}$ and $\boldsymbol{\delta}$ vectors without the z_k variable, the average such effect based on the sample is

$$E\left[\frac{\Delta_{z_k} \exp\{\boldsymbol{z}_i'\boldsymbol{\delta}(\tau)\}}{\Delta z_k}\right] \approx \left(e^{\hat{\delta}_k(\tau)} - 1\right) \cdot \frac{1}{n}\sum_{i=1}^n \exp\{\tilde{\boldsymbol{z}}_i'\widehat{\tilde{\boldsymbol{\delta}}}(\tau)\}.$$

In both cases the sign of the coefficient $\hat{\delta}_k(\tau)$ determines whether the covariate under examination tends to increase (positive sign) or decrease (negative sign) inefficiency.

These averages are contained in Table 11.5. The largest effects, across quantiles belong to recreational income (Z_1) and agricultural income (Z_2). The recreational marginal effects being positive suggest that higher levels of this income source lead to larger levels of production inefficiency while higher levels of agricultural income leads to smaller levels of inefficiency, on average.

Table 11.5: Estimates of marginal effects on inefficiency from the nonlinear quantile stochastic frontier across various quantiles.

	$\tau = 0.5$	$\tau = 0.6$	$\tau = 0.7$	$\tau = 0.8$	$\tau = 0.9$
Z_1	0.129	0.185	0.225	0.155	0.127
Z_2	−0.024	−0.031	−0.041	−0.078	−0.286
Z_3	−0.003	−0.010	−0.008	−0.003	−0.060
Z_4	−0.002	−0.003	−0.016	−0.031	−0.024
Z_5	−0.002	−0.008	−0.015	−0.028	−0.005
Z_6	0.000	−0.001	−0.002	0.004	0.003
$E[TE_z]$	0.838	0.838	0.840	0.841	0.841

The other four determinants have much smaller marginal effects across all five quantiles considered, suggesting that, on average, these four variables do not substantially influence inefficiency. Z_3 has an economically meaningful downward effect on inefficiency at $\tau = 0.9$, while for both $\tau = 0.8$ and $\tau = 0.9$, the average marginal effect for Z_4 is also efficiency increasing. Regardless of the quantile, the marginal effects for Z_6 are economically small. We also present the standard average technical efficiency scores across the forests for reference. We see that the forest owners, in this specific modeling setup are highly efficient, on average, and the average level of efficiency is stable across the quantiles. We remind the reader that this is "covariate-dependent" efficiency, per the discussion in Section 10.

Part III
For the Road

12

Challenges Ahead

At various places in this study we have mentioned or hinted at unfinished business. Here we collect and present open issues that relate to asymptotic theory, statistical testing, accounting for panel data and nonparametric estimation, as interesting topics for future theoretical breakthroughs.

Inference for the Corrected Q-Estimator

In order to strengthen the reliability of the Corrected Q-estimator a worthy endeavor would be to determine its asymptotic distribution. This should start with the asymptotic distribution of the centered quantile residuals, and proceed to determine the distribution of the individual coefficient estimators, *a la* Olson *et al.* (1980), while Coelli (1995) could inspire adjusted significance tests.

Testing the Distributional Assumption Using Quantiles

We provide here the preliminaries on distributional specification tests based on quantiles.

Using Conditional Quantiles of the Error Components

The Production Frontier. Here the composite error term is $\varepsilon_i = v_i - u_i$. We consider the conditional quantile relation, for some τ, $q_{v|\varepsilon}(\tau|\varepsilon_i) \equiv G_{v|\varepsilon}^{-1}(\tau)$. For the same τ, we have

$$\Pr(u_i \le q_{u|\varepsilon}(\tau|\varepsilon_i) | \varepsilon_i) = \tau$$
$$\implies \Pr(v_i - \varepsilon_i \le q_{u|\varepsilon}(\tau|\varepsilon_i) | \varepsilon_i) = \tau$$
$$\implies \Pr(v_i \le \varepsilon_i + q_{u|\varepsilon}(\tau|\varepsilon_i) | \varepsilon_i) = \tau$$
$$\implies G_{v|\varepsilon}\left(\varepsilon_i + q_{u|\varepsilon}(\tau|\varepsilon_i)\right) = \tau.$$

Applying $G_{v|\varepsilon}^{-1}(\cdot)$ to both sides of the expression and rearranging, we obtain

$$\varepsilon_i = q_{v|\varepsilon}(\tau|\varepsilon_i) - q_{u|\varepsilon}(\tau|\varepsilon_i).$$

Essentially the same principle that we saw in Section 2 applies here.[1]

Consider then for the left-hand side the consistent predictor $\hat{\varepsilon}_i(\hat{\tau}_{DF})$ and assume distributions for the right-hand side. Under the null hypothesis of correct specification, it will be the case that

$$|\hat{\varepsilon}_i(\hat{\tau}_{DF}) - (\hat{q}_{v|\varepsilon}(\tau|\varepsilon_i) - \hat{q}_{u|\varepsilon}(\tau|\varepsilon_i))| \underset{H_0}{\longrightarrow_p} 0, \quad \forall i, \quad \forall \tau.$$

Notice that this should hold for every i and for every τ, and so it can form the basis for a formal statistical test.

The Cost Frontier. The expression for a cost frontier changes, because we have to transform a tail probability to a cumulative probability. Here the composite error term is $\varepsilon_i = v_i + u_i$, and we consider the conditional quantile relation, $q_{v|\varepsilon}(1-\tau|\varepsilon_i) \equiv G_{v|\varepsilon}^{-1}(1-\tau)$. For the same τ, we have

$$\Pr(u_i \le q_{u|\varepsilon}(\tau|\varepsilon_i) | \varepsilon_i) = \tau$$
$$\implies \Pr(\varepsilon_i - v_i \le q_{u|\varepsilon}(\tau|\varepsilon_i) | \varepsilon_i) = \tau$$
$$\implies 1 - \Pr(v_i \le \varepsilon_i - q_{u|\varepsilon}(\tau|\varepsilon_i) | \varepsilon_i) = \tau$$
$$\implies G_{v|\varepsilon}\left(\varepsilon_i - q_{u|\varepsilon}(\tau|\varepsilon_i)\right) = 1 - \tau.$$

---
[1] Note the interplay between realizations, *conditional* quantiles, and additivity.

Following as before we have, in the case of a cost frontier,
$$\varepsilon_i = q_{v\,|\,\varepsilon}(1-\tau\,|\,\varepsilon_i) + q_{u\,|\,\varepsilon}(\tau\,|\,\varepsilon_i).$$
Here, under correct specification we obtain the statistic
$$|\widehat{\varepsilon}_i(\widehat{\tau}_{DF}) - (\hat{q}_{v\,|\,\varepsilon}(1-\tau\,|\,\varepsilon_i) + \hat{q}_{u\,|\,\varepsilon}(\tau\,|\,\varepsilon_i))| \underset{H_0}{\longrightarrow_p} 0, \quad \forall\,i,\ \ \forall\,\tau.$$

Using Estimates of the Constant Term of the Regression at Different Quantile Probabilities

As we have said, the importance of having a consistent predictor series for the residuals and the location of the deterministic frontier, makes the execution of the Q-estimator at different quantiles problematic in SFA. But we can use multiple-quantiles estimation to construct another specification test.

Assume that we estimate the deterministic frontier as described earlier, and so we have
$$\hat{\alpha}(\widehat{\tau}_{DF}) \longrightarrow_p \alpha.$$
Then by executing the Q-estimator at other τ values $\tau_1, \ldots, \tau_j, \ldots \tau_m$, we can obtain the series
$$\hat{\alpha}(\tau_j) - \hat{\alpha}(\widehat{\tau}_{DF}) = q_\varepsilon(\tau_j) + o_p(1), \quad j = 1, \ldots, m.$$
At the same time, we can compute estimates for these quantiles by using the assumed distribution for the composite error term,
$$G_\varepsilon^{-1}(\tau_j; \hat{\theta}) = q_\varepsilon(\tau_j) + o_p(1),$$
where $\hat{\theta}$ represents the vector of estimated distribution parameters. Under the null hypothesis of correct specification we will have
$$|G_\varepsilon^{-1}(\tau_j; \hat{\theta}) - \alpha(\widehat{\tau}_j) + \alpha(\widehat{\tau}_{DF})| \underset{H_0}{\longrightarrow_p} 0, \quad \forall\,j.$$

This is another route to construct a specification test for the distributional assumptions, here using the quantiles of the error term and multiple-quantiles estimation by the Q-estimator, perhaps along the lines of a Kolmogorov-Smirnov approach, and the use of the suprema of these absolute values. The asymptotic theory for these tests would likely be complicated and, since we have to use estimated quantities, bootstrapping will be needed to construct variances and/or critical values.

Handling Panel Data

We briefly review here the small literature related to quantile regression in a panel data setting, in order to highlight the challenges that arise but also the avenues that one could take. Quantile regression with panel data is conceptually and technically complicated, and still very much a rather unsettled endeavor.

The wheels of research started to turn many years after the introduction of quantile regression, with Koenker (2004) who presented a fixed-effects model where the individual effects were time-invariant, not depending on the conditioning quantile probability, and therefore representing only a location shift, just an individual intercept, and not a distributional shift. The author deployed a weighted and penalized Q-estimator where we pool and weight sample information over several τ's in order to improve the estimation of the individual effects. But the model is applicable conditional on a single τ also (at the researcher's peril). Lamarche (2010) established further that there exists an optimal value for the regularization parameter attached to the penalty term and provided the related formula. Galvao and Montes-Rojas (2010) extended the penalized fixed effects model to a dynamic setting while Galvao (2011) revisited the dynamic model but this time without a penalty term. Harding and Lamarche (2009) considered a model with endogeneity and IV estimation where the individual effect is estimated on its own with the use of the two-stage method of Chernozhukov and Hansen (2008).

Kato *et al.* (2012) examined carefully the asymptotic theory for the fixed effects Q-estimator for large-N/large-T panels (for the static and for the dynamic case). A main finding is that asymptotic Normality requires the T-dimension to grow much faster than the N-dimension. Galvao and Kato (2016) smoothed the objective function and obtain asymptotic Normality when N and T grow at the same rate. A bias remains in the asymptotic mean and they propose a bias-reduction scheme.

Graham *et al.* (2018) presented a quantile correlated random coefficients panel data model (in a "fixed-effects" approach). Gu and Volgushev (2019) examined a model with grouped fixed effects. Zhang *et al.* (2019) had similar concerns and proposed a new quantile-regression-based clustering method for panel data. These approaches could link to an SFA model with group-frontiers and the meta-frontier approach.

Abrevaya and Dahl (2008) developed an early model with random effects, where the individual effect is partly a function of the regressors, which is essentially the formulation of Mundlak (1978). Rosen (2012) was concerned with relaxing the i.i.d assumption related to the error term across the temporal dimension. He shows that, left completely unrestricted, dependence leads to loss of identification. He derives a set of restrictions weaker than full independence that restore identification.

Canay (2011) started with a random-coefficients panel data model that is a mean-conditional model with a mean-independent and conditionally heteroskedastic error term. After estimating the individual effect, he proposed a quantile regression where we subtract the estimated individual effect from the dependent variable. We note that in a SFM the estimate of the individual effect will include also the non-zero mean of the composite error term, hence it is not clear how one could proceed from there.

Besstremyannaya and Golovan (2019) detected two errors in Canay (2011). One relates to the needed rates of convergence to infinity of the two panel dimensions. They show that the condition that guarantees asymptotically valid inference requires a much higher growth of the T dimension than what Canay asserted, leading again to the conclusion that quantile regression requires long panels to be trusted. The second error relates to the estimation and inference of the constant term of the model. Chen and Huo (2021) elaborated further on the problems that plague Canay's model and estimation method, and offer an alternative "simple" approach, by combining the first step of Canay's estimator with a "smoothed quantile regression" as proposed in Galvao and Kato (2016). This second step is no longer a linear programming problem but a non-linear minimization one, albeit estimating fewer parameters than in Galvao and Kato's method.

A main lesson from all these studies is that once we move away from the most naive dependence structure (i.i.d data across both dimensions of the panel), established techniques like data transformation do not work: in the complete i.i.d. case, we could certainly apply first-differencing to obtain estimates of the slope regression coefficients using the Q-estimator, estimates that would be the same across quantiles. But then again, the complete i.i.d. case essentially reduces panel data to a large cross-sectional sample.[2] In an i.i.d.-fixed effects setting we exploit neither the panel structure nor the potential of the Q-estimator for different results per different quantile. Once some form of quantile dependence is allowed, the quantile regression coefficients will differ per τ, and then we have to work with untransformed data, and/or multiple-stage procedures.

A second message is that the asymptotics of the Q-estimator with panel data are opaque and need special attention and examination in more depth than usual.

A third result is that currently, the estimators need long panels to claim asymptotic validity, in fact samples where the temporal dimension dominates the cross-sectional. This limits their practical reliability. In this respect the sensible approach of Galvao and Kato (2016) that restored balance between the two dimensions and attempts to correct for the resulting bias looks promising.

Finally, the case of a quantile-dependent individual effect has been left essentially unexplored, or put aside by treating models and estimators "conditional on the individual effect" (which then can be conveniently left uncharacterized).[3] Only the model of Abrevaya and Dahl (2008) of those mentioned above treat the issue directly, by making the individual effect partly dependent on the regressors. This leads to a quantile-dependent individual effect. It also provides an obvious

---

[2]This was the case with Knox *et al.* (2007) that we presented in Section 4, which applied standard quantile regression on a pooled panel data sample.

[3]Machado and Silva (2019) proposed a novel "quantiles via moments" approach to estimate panel data models with individual effects that are, eventually, quantile-dependent.

connection to the "determinants of inefficiency" SFA model, at least if we are willing to consider a set of covariates (possibly including the regressors) that operate as "determinants of the individual effect".

In the SFA literature, Laporte and Dass (2016) and Hsu *et al.* (2017) made a first attempt at applying panel-data quantile regression, initially using simulated data and in the second article an empirical data set. They equated the individual effect with inefficiency, and then applied both the Schmidt and Sickles (1984) approach to compute inefficiency, and also the Mundlak (1978) approach where the individual effect is a function of regressors. Identifying inefficiency with the individual effect has been criticized in the literature, see for example Greene (2005).

Colombi *et al.* (2014) have proposed a four component model that nests most of the SF panel data models that have been published. Their model separates the individual effect from time-invariant inefficiency, and also includes time varying inefficiency and stochastic noise (hence four components).[4] By nesting the restricted formulations, this four component model also provides a useful compact typology for researchers to decide, conceptually and structurally in the first place, what is more suitable for each applied study. We should also anticipate that quantile estimation methods may have different particularities, different asymptotics and different results as we choose different assumptions on the unobservables of a SFM with panel data.

Nonparametric Methods

The discussion so far has focused on parametric specification of the production frontier. However, there have been major developments in the area of nonparametric quantile estimation and those methods could also be deployed here to estimate the frontier. See Li and Racine (2007) for a textbook treatment of nonparametric quantile regression. One early paper in this area is Wang *et al.* (2014). The authors used convexification and monotonization to construct a piecewise linear representation of the true, unknown quantile process. Consequently, if the axioms of production underlying these restrictions do not hold then

---
[4]Under specific distributional assumptions the model has a Closed Skew Normal likelihood.

this estimator will not be consistent. An alternative approach, which is nonparametric in nature, but does not rely on axioms of production to pull out the shape of the frontier is kernel smoothing. This is akin in the conditional mean setting to the work of Fan et al. (1996) (see Parmeter and Kumbhakar, 2014, for a review).

In the presence of determinants of inefficiency, one problem with direct nonparametric quantile estimation is that the object that is returned is not a quantile frontier, but a conditional quantile. Consider the nonparametric quantile estimator of Li and Racine (2008). With this approach one would estimate the conditional CDF of output (or cost) conditional on both x and z. However, because the quantile is recovered by inverting the estimated conditional CDF, there is no way to distinguish between the impact of x on the frontier and z on inefficiency.

An alternative approach would be to try to follow the setup of Tran and Tsionas (2009) and Parmeter et al. (2017) which exploits the partial linear structure of the stochastic frontier model in the presence of determinants of inefficiency. This would entail estimation of the quantile model

$$y_i = x_i'\beta(\tau) + \sigma(z_i, \tau)\varepsilon_i, \qquad (12.1)$$

where $\text{Var}(\varepsilon_i) = 1$ and so $\sigma(z_i, \tau)$ is the standard deviation of the composite error, something that does not allow separate identification of the distribution parameters of the components of ε_i.

For this "partly linear" setup a quantile estimator based on B-splines (Wang et al., 2009) can be constructed. Let $N = N_n$ be the number of interior knots and let q be the spline order. Divide $[0, 1]$ (we can always rescale any of our variables that do not live on $[0, 1]$ accordingly) into $(N + 1)$ subintervals $I_j = [r_j, r_{j+1}), j = 0, \ldots, N - 1$, $I_N = [r_N, 1]$, where $\{r_j\}_{j=1}^{N}$ is a sequence of interior knots, given as

$$r_{-(q-1)} = \cdots = r_0 = 0 < r_1 < \cdots < r_N < 1 = r_{N+1} = \cdots = r_{N+q}.$$

Define the q-th order B-spline basis as $B_{s,q} = \{B_j(x_s) : 1 - q \leq j \leq N\}'$ (de Boor, 2001, Page 89). Let $G_{s,q} = G_{s,q}^{(q-2)}$ be the space spanned by $B_{s,q}$, and let G_q be the tensor product of $G_{1,q}, \ldots, G_{d,q}$, which is the space of functions spanned by

$$\begin{aligned}\mathcal{B}_q(z) &= B_{1,q} \otimes \cdots \otimes B_{d,q} \\ &= \left[\left\{\prod_{s=1}^{d} B_{j_s,q}(z_s) : 1-q \leq j_s \leq N, 1 \leq s \leq d\right\}'\right]_{K_n \times 1} \\ &= \left[\{\mathcal{B}_{j_1,\ldots,j_d,q}(z) : 1-q \leq j_s \leq N, 1 \leq s \leq d\}'\right]_{K_n \times 1},\end{aligned}$$

where $z = (z_1, \ldots, z_d)'$ and $K_n = (N+q)^d$. Let $\mathbf{B}_q = [\{\mathcal{B}_q(z_1), \ldots, \mathcal{B}_q(z_n)\}']_{n \times K_n}$. Then $\sigma(z, \tau)$ can be approximated by $\mathcal{B}_q(z)'\theta$, where θ is a $K_n \times 1$ vector. With this notation in tow we can estimate our partly linear quantile stochastic frontier model as

$$\min_{\beta,\theta} \sum_{i=1}^{n} \rho_\tau \left(\frac{y_i - x_i'\beta(\tau)}{\mathcal{B}_q(z_i)'\theta(\tau)} \right). \tag{12.2}$$

To our knowledge this type of an approach has not appeared in the quantile estimation literature but does follow the parametric approach in Jung *et al.* (2015). The theoretical properties of this estimator are left for future work.

13

Summary and Concluding Remarks

In this work we started a bit grimly, sounding the alarm and showing the incompatibilities that exist between quantile regression and SFA, by using theory but also by reviewing published applied studies (Sections 2–6). But then, we provided new estimation and inference tools that surmount these obstacles and allow the valid use of quantile regression and the quantile approach more generally in SFA (Sections 7–11). Specifically, we developed the quantile-based Corrected Q-estimator, that is simple to implement and performed well in the empirical illustration of Section 11, and, for the first time in the SFA literature, we constructed valid quantile-dependent measures of efficiency, both at the sample level but also for individual observations. We showed how the availability of determinants of inefficiency in a data set can be exploited by the implementation of a non-linear quantile model. We also proved an important theoretical result as regards the composed error term of stochastic frontier analysis: large positive values of the composed error in a production model have a large probability of containing *low* values of inefficiency, when noise and inefficiency are independent. This provides a link between conditional and unconditional quantiles that could be further explored... alongside the many other open research topics, that we have mainly collected in Section 12. The empirical application of Section 11 we believe vindicates our belief that the quantile approach is an interesting and useful path to take in order to enhance stochastic frontier and efficiency analysis. Yes, the approach needs to be modified; yes, there are still many things we do not yet know; but there are illuminating ways to do quantile-based applied stochastic frontier and efficiency analysis *now*, while we expand this frontier also.

References

Abrevaya, J. and C. M. Dahl (2008). "The effects of birth inputs on birthweight: Evidence from quantile estimation on panel data". *Journal of Business & Economic Statistics*. 26(4): 379–397.

Aigner, D. J., C. A. K. Lovell, and P. Schmidt (1977). "Formulation and estimation of stochastic frontier production functions". *Journal of Econometrics*. 6(1): 21–37.

Amemiya, T. (1982). "Two stage least absolute deviations estimators". *Econometrica*. 50(3): 689–711.

Amsler, C., A. Papadopoulos, and P. Schmidt (2021). "Evaluating the CDF of the Skew normal distribution". *Empirical Economics*. 60: 3171–3202.

Aragon, Y., A. Daouia, and C. Thomas-Agnan (2005). "Nonparametric Frontier estimation: A conditional quantile-based approach". *Econometric Theory*. 21(2): 358–389.

Assaf, A. G., M. G. Tsionas, and F. Kock (2020). "Dynamic quantile stochastic frontier models". *International Journal of Hospitality Management*. 89: 102588.

Azzalini, A. (1986). "Further results on a class of distributions which includes the normal ones". *Statistica*. 46(2): 199–208.

Azzalini, A. and A. Capitanio (2014). *The Skew-Normal and Related Families*. Cambridge University Press.

Badunenko, O. and D. J. Henderson (2021). "Production analysis with asymmetric error". MPRA Paper No. 110888. URL: https://mpra.ub.uni-muenchen.de/110888.

Battese, G. E. and T. J. Coelli (1988). "Prediction of firm-level technical efficiencies with a generalized frontier production function and panel data". *Journal of Econometrics*. 38: 387–399.

Behr, A. (2010). "Quantile regression for robust bank efficiency score estimation". *European Journal of Operational Research*. 200: 568–581.

Bera, A. K., A. F. Galvao, G. V. Montes-Rojas, and S. Y. Park (2016). "Asymmetric Laplace regression: Maximum likelihood, maximum entropy and quantile regression". *Journal of Econometric Methods*. 5: 79–101.

Berger, A. N. and D. B. Humphrey (1991). "The dominance of inefficiencies over scale and product mix economies in banking". *Journal of Monetary Economics*. 28(1): 117–148.

Bernini, C., M. Freo, and A. Gardini (2004). "Quantile estimation of frontier production function". *Empirical Economics*. 29: 373–381.

Bernstein, D., C. F. Parmeter, and M. Tsionas (2021). On Bayesian quantile estimation of the stochastic Frontier model. Mimeo.

Besstremyannaya, G. and S. Golovan (2019). "Reconsideration of a simple approach to quantile regression for panel data". *The Econometrics Journal*. 22(3): 292–308.

Bonanno, G., D. De Giovanni, and F. Domma (2015). "The 'wrong skewness' problem: A re-specification of stochastic frontiers". *Journal of Productivity Analysis*. 47(1): 49–64.

Buchinsky, M. (1998). "Recent advances in quantile regression models: a practical guideline for empirical research". *Journal of Human Resources*: 88–126.

Canay, I. A. (2011). "A simple approach to quantile regression for panel data". *The Econometrics Journal*. 14: 368–386.

Capitanio, A. (2010). "On the approximation of the tail probability of the scalar skew-normal distribution". *Metron*. 68(3): 299–308.

Chen, L. and Y. Huo (2021). "A simple estimator for quantile panel data models using smoothed quantile regressions". *The Econometrics Journal*. 24(2): 247–263.

References

Chernozhukov, V., I. Fernández-Val, and A. Galichon (2010). "Quantile and probability curves without crossing". *Econometrica*. 78(3): 1093–1125.

Chernozhukov, V. and C. Hansen (2008). "Instrumental variable quantile regression: A robust inference approach". *Journal of Econometrics*. 142(1): 379–398.

Chidmi, B., D. Solís, and V. E. Cabrera (2011). "Analyzing the sources of technical efficiency among heterogeneous dairy farms: A quantile regression approach". *Journal of Development and Agricultural Economics*. 3(7): 318–324.

Coelli, T. J. (1995). "Estimators and hypothesis tests for a stochastic Frontier function: A Monte Carlo analysis". *Journal of Productivity Analysis*. 6(4): 247–268.

Colombi, R., S. Kumbhakar, G. Martini, and G. Vittadini (2014). "Closed-skew normality in stochastic Frontiers with individual effects and long/short-run efficiency". *Journal of Productivity Analysis*. 42(2): 123–136.

Daouia, A. and L. Simar (2007). "Nonparametric efficiency analysis: A multivariate conditional quantile approach". *Journal of Econometrics*. 140(2): 375–400.

David, F. N. (1953). "A note on the evaluation of the multivariate Normal integral". *Biometrika*. 40(3–4): 458–459.

de Boor, C. (2001). *A Practical Guide to Splines*. New York: Springer.

Fan, Y., Q. Li, and A. Weersink (1996). "Semiparametric estimation of stochastic production frontier models". *Journal of Business & Economic Statistics*. 14(4): 460–468.

Firpo, S., N. M. Fortin, and T. Lemieux (2009). "Unconditional quantile regressions". *Econometrica*. 77(3): 953–973.

Fitzenberger, B., R. Koenker, and J. A. F. Machado (2002). *Economic Applications of Quantile Regression*. Springer Verlag.

Fitzenberger, B., R. Koenker, J. Machado, and B. Melly (2022). "Economic applications of quantile regression 2.0". *Empirical Economics*. 62(1): 1–6.

Frumento, P. and M. Bottai (2016). "Parametric modeling of quantile regression coefficient functions". *Biometrics*. 72(1): 74–84.

Fusco, E., R. Benedetti, and F. Vidoli (2022). "Stochastic frontier estimation through parametric modelling of quantile regression coefficients". *Empirical Economics*. URL: https://doi.org/10.1007/s00181-022-02273-x.

Galvao, A. F. (2011). "Quantile regression for dynamic panel data with fixed effects". *Journal of Econometrics*. 164(1): 142–157.

Galvao, A. F. and K. Kato (2016). "Smoothed quantile regression for panel data". *Journal of Econometrics*. 193(1): 92–112.

Galvao, A. F. and G. V. Montes-Rojas (2010). "Penalized quantile regression for dynamic panel data". *Journal of Statistical Planning and Inference*. 140(11): 3476–3497.

Godfrey, L. G. and C. D. Orme (1991). "Testing for skewness of regression disturbances". *Economics Letters*. 37(1): 31–34.

Goldberger, A. S. (1968). "The interpretation and estimation of Cobb-Douglas functions". *Econometrica*. 36(3/4): 464–472.

Graham, B. S., J. Hahn, A. Poirier, and J. L. Powell (2018). "A quantile correlated random coefficients panel data model". *Journal of Econometrics*. 206(2): 305–335.

Greene, W. H. (1980). "Maximum likelihood estimation of econometric frontier functions". *Journal of Econometrics*. 13(1): 27–56.

Greene, W. H. (2005). "Fixed and random effects in stochastic frontier models". *Journal of Productivity Analysis*. 23(1): 7–32.

Gregg, D. and J. Rolfe (2016). "The value of environment across efficiency quantiles: A conditional regression quantiles analysis of rangelands beef production in north Eastern Australia". *Ecological Economics*. 128: 44–54.

Griliches, Z. (1957). "Specification bias in estimates of production functions". *Journal of Farm Economics*. 39(1): 8–20.

Gu, J. and S. Volgushev (2019). "Panel data quantile regression with grouped fixed effects". *Journal of Econometrics*. 213(1): 68–91.

Gupta, R. D. and D. Kundu (1999). "Generalized exponential distributions". *Australian and New Zealand Journal of Statistics*. 41(2): 173–188.

Harding, M. and C. Lamarche (2009). "A quantile regression approach for estimating panel data models using instrumental variables". *Economics Letters*. 104(3): 133–135.

Horrace, W. C. and C. F. Parmeter (2018). "A Laplace stochastic frontier model". *Econometric Reviews*. 37: 260–280.

Horrace, W. C., C. F. Parmeter, and I. Wright (2021). On asymmetry and quantiles in the stochastic Frontier model. Mimeo.

Hsu, A., A. R. Dass, W. Bert, P. Coyte, and A. Laporte (2017). "Efficiency estimation with panel quantile regression: An application using longitudinal data from nursing homes in Ontario, Canada". *Working Paper* No. 170003. Canadian Centre for health economics.

Jondrow, J., C. A. K. Lovell, I. S. Materov, and P. Schmidt (1982). "On the estimation of technical efficiency in the stochastic frontier production function model". *Journal of Econometrics*. 19(2/3): 233–238.

Jradi, S., C. F. Parmeter, and J. Ruggiero (2019). "Quantile estimation of the stochastic Frontier model". *Economics Letters*. 182: 15–18.

Jradi, S., C. F. Parmeter, and J. Ruggiero (2021). "Quantile Estimation of Stochastic Frontiers with the Normal-Exponential Specification". *European Journal of Operational Research*. 295(2): 475–483.

Jradi, S. and J. Ruggiero (2019). "Stochastic data envelopment analysis: A quantile regression approach to estimate the production frontier". *European Journal of Operational Research*. 278: 385–393.

Jung, Y., Y. Lee, and S. N. MacEachern (2015). "Efficient quantile regression for heteroscedastic models". *Journal of Statistical Computation and Simulation*. 85(13): 2548–2568.

Kaditi, E. A. and E. I. Nitsi (2010). "Applying regression quantiles to farm efficiency estimation". *Discussion Paper* No. 112. Centre of Planning and Economic Research (KEPE). URL: https://www.kepe.gr/index.php/en/research/recent-publications/discussion-papers.

Kato, K., A. F. Galvao, and G. V. Montes-Rojas (2012). "Asymptotics for panel quantile regression models with individual effects". *Journal of Econometrics*. 170(1): 76–91.

Knox, K. J., E. C. Blankmeyer, and J. R. Stutzman (2007). "Technical efficiency in Texan nursing facilities: A stochastic production forntier approach". *Journal of Economics and Finance*. 31(1): 75–86.

Koenker, R. (2004). "Quantile regression for longitudinal data". *Journal of Multivariate Analysis*. 91(1): 74–89.

Koenker, R. (2005). *Quantile Regression*. Cambridge University Press.

Koenker, R. and G. Bassett (1978). "Regression quantiles". *Econometrica*. 46(1): 33–50.

Koenker, R. and G. Bassett (1982). "Robust tests for heteroscedasticity based on regression quantiles". *Econometrica*. 50: 43–61.

Komunjer, I. (2005). "Quasi-maximum likelihood estimation for conditional quantiles". *Journal of Econometrics*. 128(1): 137–164.

Kumbhakar, S. C., R. Amundsveen, H. M. Kvile, and G. Lien (2015). "Scale economies, technical change and efficiency in Norwegian electricity distribution, 1998–2010". *Journal of Productivity Analysis*. 43(3): 295–305.

Kumbhakar, S. C. and C. A. K. Lovell (2000). *Stochastic Frontier Analysis*. Cambridge University Press.

Kumbhakar, S. C., C. F. Parmeter, and V. Zelenyuk (2020). "Stochastic Frontier analysis: Foundations and advances II". In: *Handbook of Production Economics*. Ed. by S. Ray, R. Chambers, and S. C. Kumbhakar. Vol. 1. Springer.

Kumbhakar, S. C. and H.-J. Wang (2010). "Estimation of technical inefficiency in production Frontier models using cross-sectional data". *Indian Economic Review*. 45(2): 7–77.

Lamarche, C. (2010). "Robust penalized quantile regression estimation for panel data". *Journal of Econometrics*. 157(2): 396–408.

Land, K. C., C. K. Lovell, and S. Thore (1993). "Chance-constrained data envelopment analysis". *Managerial and Decision Economics*. 14(6): 541–554.

Laporte, A. and A. R. Dass (2016). "The use of panel quantile regression for efficiency measurement: Insights from Monte Carlo simulations". *Working Paper* No. 160005. Canadian Centre for health economics.

Lee, T.-H., A. Ullah, and H. Wang (2018). "The second-order bias of quantile estimators". *Economics Letters*. 173: 143–147.

Li, Q. and J. Racine (2007). *Nonparametric Econometrics: Theory and Practice*. Princeton University Press.

Li, Q. and J. S. Racine (2008). "Nonparametric estimation of conditional CDF and quantile functions with mixed categorical and continuous data". *Journal of Business & Economic Statistics*. 26(4): 423–434.

- Lien, G., S. Størdal, and S. Baardsen (2007). "Technical efficiency in timber production and effects of other income sources". *Small-Scale Forestry*. 6: 65–78.
- Liu, C., A. Laporte, and B. S. Ferguson (2008). "The quantile regression approach to efficiency measurement: Insights from Monte Carlo simulations". *Health Economics*. 17: 1073–1087.
- Liu, J. and H. A. David (1989). "Quantiles of sums and expected values of ordered sums". *Australian Journal of Statistics*. 31(3): 469–474.
- Machado, J. A. and J. S. Silva (2019). "Quantiles via moments". *Journal of Econometrics*. 213(1): 145–173.
- Maneejuk, P. and W. Yamaka (2021). "Copula-based stochastic Frontier quantile model with unknown quantile". In: *Data Science for Financial Econometrics*. Ed. by N. Ngoc Thach, V. Kreinovich, and N. D. Trung. Cham: Springer International Publishing. 445–458.
- Martins-Filho, C. and F. Yao (2008). "A smooth nonparametric conditional quantile frontier estimator". *Journal of Econometrics*. 143(2): 317–333.
- Meeusen, W. and J. van den Broeck (1977). "Efficiency estimation from Cobb-Douglas production functions with composed error". *International Economic Review*. 18(2): 435–444.
- Mundlak, Y. (1978). "On the pooling of time series and cross section data". *Econometrica*. 46(1): 69–85.
- Nelsen, R. B. (1993). "Some concepts of bivariate symmetry". *Journal of Nonparametric Statistics*. 3(1): 95–101.
- Oberhofer, W. (1982). "The consistency of nonlinear regression minimizing the L1-norm". *The Annals of Statistics*: 316–319.
- Olson, J. A., P. Schmidt, and D. A. Waldman (1980). "A Monte Carlo study of estimators of stochastic frontier production functions". *Journal of Econometrics*. 13: 67–82.
- Ondrich, J. and J. Ruggiero (2001). "Efficiency measurement in the stochastic frontier model". *European Journal of Operational Research*. 129(3): 434–442.
- Papadopoulos, A. (2021a). "Measuring the effect of management on production: a two-tier stochastic frontier approach". *Empirical Economics*. 60: 3011–3041.

Papadopoulos, A. (2021b). "Stochastic frontier models using the Generalized Exponential distribution". *Journal of Productivity Analysis.* 55(1): 15–29.

Papadopoulos, A. (2022a). "The noise error component in Stochastic Frontier Analysis". Paper presented at EWEPA XVII, Porto, Portugal.

Papadopoulos, A. (2022b). "Trade liberalization and growth: a quantile moderator for Hoyos'(2021) replication study of Estevadeordal and Taylor (2013)". *Empirical Economics.* 63: 549–563.

Papadopoulos, A. and C. F. Parmeter (2021). "Type II failure and specification testing in the stochastic Frontier model". *European Journal of Operational Research.* 293(3): 990–1001.

Parmeter, C. F. (2021). "Is it MOLS or COLS?" *Tech. rep.* University of Oviedo, Department of Economics, Oviedo Efficiency Group (OEG).

Parmeter, C. F. and S. C. Kumbhakar (2014). "Efficiency analysis: A primer on recent advances". *Foundations and Trends in Econometrics.* 7(3–4): 191–385.

Parmeter, C. F., H.-J. Wang, and S. C. Kumbhakar (2017). "Nonparametric estimation of the determinants of inefficiency". *Journal of Productivity Analysis.* 47(3): 205–221.

Paul, S. and S. Shankar (2018). "On estimating efficiency effects in a stochastic frontier model". *European Journal of Operational Research.* 271(2): 769–774.

Poiraud-Casanova, S. and C. Thomas-Agnan (2000). "About monotone regression quantiles". *Statistics & Probability Letters.* 48(1): 101–104.

Rosen, A. M. (2012). "Set identification via quantile restrictions in short panels". *Journal of Econometrics.* 166(1): 127–137.

Schennach, S. M. (2005). "Bayesian exponentially tilted empirical likelihood". *Biometrika*: 31–46.

Schmidt, P. and R. C. Sickles (1984). "Production Frontiers and panel data". *Journal of Business & Economic Statistics.* 2(2): 367–374.

Sickles, R. C. and V. Zelenyuk (2019). *Measurement of Productivity and Efficiency.* Cambridge University Press.

Stead, A. D., P. Wheat, and W. H. Greene (2022a). "Quantile regression estimation of the stochastic frontier model: Choice of quantile and robustness". Paper presented at EWEPA XVII, Porto, Portugal.

Stead, A. D., P. Wheat, and W. H. Greene (2022b). "Robustness in stochastic Frontier analysis". In: *Advanced Mathematical Methods in Economic Efficiency Analysis, Lecture Notes in Economics and Mathematical Systems*. Ed. by P. Macedo, V. F. Moutinho, and M. Madaleno. Cham: Springer International Publishing.

Stigler, S. M. (1980). "Stigler's law of eponymy". *Transactions of the New York Academy of Sciences*. 39(1 Series II): 147–157.

Tran, K. C. and E. G. Tsionas (2009). "Estimation of nonparametric inefficiency effects stochastic frontier models with an application to British manufacturing". *Economic Modelling*. 26: 904–909.

Tsionas, E. G., A. G. Assaf, and A. Andrikopoulos (2020). "Quantile stochastic frontier models with endogeneity". *Economics Letters*. 188: 108964.

Tsionas, M. G. (2020a). "Quantile stochastic frontiers". *European Journal of Operational Research*. 282(3): 1177–1184.

Tsionas, M. G. (2020b). "Bounded rationality and thick frontiers in stochastic frontier analysis". *European Journal of Operational Research*. 284(2): 762–768.

Van den Broeck, J., G. Koop, J. Osiewalski, and M. F. Steel (1994). "Stochastic frontier models: A Bayesian perspective". *Journal of Econometrics*. 61(2): 273–303.

Wang, H.-J. and P. Schmidt (2002). "One-step and two-step estimation of the effects of exogenous variables on technical efficiency levels". *Journal of Productivity Analysis*. 18: 129–144.

Wang, H. J., Z. Zhu, and J. Zhou (2009). "Quantile regression in partially linear varying coefficient models". *The Annals of Statistics*. 37(6B): 3841–3866.

Wang, W. S. and P. Schmidt (2009). "On the distribution of estimated technical efficiency in stochastic frontier models". *Journal of Econometrics*. 148(1): 36–45.

Wang, Y., S. Wang, C. Dang, and W. Ge (2014). "Nonparametric quantile frontier estimation under shape restriction". *European Journal of Operational Research*. 232(3): 671–678.

Watson, R. and I. Gordon (1986). "On quantiles of sums". *Australian Journal of Statistics*. 28(2): 192–199.

Wei, Z., X. Zhu, and T. Wang (2021). "The extended skew-normal-based stochastic frontier model with a solution to 'wrong skewness' problem". *Statistics*. 55(6): 1387–1406.

Wichitaksorn, N., S. B. Choy, and R. Gerlach (2014). "A generalized class of skew distributions and associated robust quantile regression models". *Canadian Journal of Statistics*. 42(4): 579–596.

Wüthrich, K. (2020). "A comparison of two quantile models with endogeneity". *Journal of Business & Economic Statistics*. 38(2): 443–456.

Zeebari, Z. (2021). "Conditional quantile estimators of unit inefficiency in stochastic frontier analysis with application to electricity distribution market". *Paper presented at the 1st Virtual African Productivity Conference.*

Zhang, N., X. Huang, and Y. Liu (2021). "The cost of low-carbon transition for China's coal-fired power plants: A quantile frontier approach". *Technological Forecasting and Social Change*. 169: 120809.

Zhang, Y., H. J. Wang, and Z. Zhu (2019). "Quantile-regression-based clustering for panel data". *Journal of Econometrics*. 213(1): 54–67.

Zhao, S. (2021). "Quantile estimation of stochastic frontier models with the normal-half normal specification: A cumulative distribution function approach". *Economics Letters*: 109998.